WHY ISRAEL CAN'T WAIT

The Coming War Between
Israel and Iran

Jerome R. Corsi, Ph.D.

**THRESHOLD
EDITIONS**

New York   London   Toronto   Sydney

Threshold Editions
A Division of Simon & Schuster, Inc.
1230 Avenue of the Americas
New York, NY 10020

First Threshold Editions trade paperback edition September 2009

THRESHOLD EDITIONS and colophon are trademarks of
Simon & Schuster, Inc.

For information about special discounts for bulk purchases,
please contact Simon & Schuster Special Sales at 1-866-506-1949
or business@simonandschuster.com.

The Simon & Schuster Speakers Bureau can bring authors to your live event.
For more information or to book an event contact the Simon & Schuster
Speakers Bureau at 1-866-248-3049 or visit our website at simonspeakers.com.

Designed by Renata Di Biase

Manufactured in the United States of America

10 9 8 7 6 5 4 3 2 1

Library of Congress Cataloging-in-Publication Data

ISBN 978-1-4391-8301-4
ISBN 978-1-4391-7190-5 (ebook)

This book is dedicated to "Dr. X," a top-secret source who guided my work and made this book possible, in recognition of his important and continuing classified contribution to the national security of the United States and the State of Israel.

In memory of David Ben-Gurion, who dared to imagine he could create the modern Jewish State of Israel.

Then they shall know that I am the Lord their God,
which caused them to be led into captivity among
     the heathen:
but I have gathered them unto their own land,
and have left none of them any more there.

—EZEKIEL 39:28

Contents

Israel's Right of Self-Defense

"For us, a nuclear-armed Iran is an existential threat," Vice Prime Minister and Minister of Strategic Affairs Moshe Yaalon told the author in a private, audio-recorded interview in his Jerusalem office, on June 14, 2009. "We have to be ready to defend ourselves."

What I was next told by Yaalon was confirmed to me by virtually all Israeli officials in the Netanyahu government whom I interviewed: Iran's nuclear weapons program is an existential threat to the survival of Israel, to the extent that Israel is reluctantly prepared to launch a preemptive military strike on Iran, with or without the approval of the United States, as early as the end of 2009 or the beginning of 2010, if the United States and the world community fail to stop Iran.

Today, Yaalon is the second-highest official in the Israeli government, outranked only by Prime Minister Benjamin Netanyahu. President Shimon Peres serves as Israel's ceremonial head of state.

Yaalon has both the military background and the experience at the highest levels of the Israeli government needed to judge realistically the threat represented by Iran's nuclear weapons program. Drafted into the Israeli Defense Forces (IDF) in 1968, he served in the Nahal Paratroop Regiment. In the Yom Kippur War in 1973, Yaalon served as a reservist. Following this, he returned to active duty in the IDF and served in the elite Special Forces Sayeret Matkal, dedicated to gathering field intelligence and conducting top-secret operations, typically behind enemy lines. Sayeret Matkal is perhaps most famous for conducting the Operation Thunderbolt raid on the Entebbe Airport on the night of July 3 and the early morning of July 4, 1976, in which Israel rescued more than one hundred Air France airline passengers being held in Uganda by Palestine Liberation Organization (PLO) terrorists. In this operation, Sayeret Matkal lost Lieutenant Colonel Yonatan "Yoni" Netanyahu, the older brother of the prime minister.

Lieutenant General Yaalon held several command positions in the IDF Paratroop Brigade and was wounded in the 1982 Lebanon war. He was named head of Military Intelligence in 1995, after which he served as the chief of staff of the Israeli Defense Forces from 2002 to 2005. Vice Prime Minister Yaalon serves as a member of the Knesset, Israel's parliament, from Likud, the party of Prime Minister Netanyahu.

When I interviewed Yaalon in Jerusalem, he had just returned from an intense week of meetings in Washington.

I asked him whether Israel has a chance to convince the White House of its position in the narrow window of opportunity before Iran has nuclear weapons capability. "The appeasement road is not going to work with Iran," he replied. "It will be Israel and the reality of the situation that will convince Washington. I cannot see any U.S. administration ready to submit to radical Islamic jihadism. President Obama told Prime Minister Netanyahu at their last meeting that he was committed not to allow a military nuclear Iran and I hope he will keep his word."[1]

I asked Yaalon directly whether he would like to tell the world in precise and unequivocal words that Israel will not accept an Iran armed with nuclear weapons, even if that involves Israel launching an attack on Iran without the White House giving a green light for a military strike.

He responded equally directly: "As bad as launching a military attack on Iran would be, the only worse choice would be to allow Iran to develop nuclear weapons. One way or another, Iran must be stopped from developing military weapons. We have the military intelligence we need to launch an effective military attack on Iran, if we have no other choice. The Israeli Defense Forces have the military capability to strike Iran's nuclear facilities successfully, if that is what we are required to do."

How much more time does Israeli intelligence estimate that Iran will need to develop nuclear weapons capability?

"In the 1990s when I was in military intelligence, we spoke

about a decade," he answered. "Today, we are speaking about months, certainly not more than a couple of years.

"Each day, Iran advances its uranium-enrichment technology," he explained. "Each day, Iran moves closer to having the quantity of enriched uranium needed to produce one bomb. That's not enough to have a true nuclear weapons capability, but Iran is well along the way."

What Is the Iranian Strategy?

"The Iranian strategy has always been to have the indigenous capability to produce all components needed for a nuclear weapons program," Yaalon said. "This involves not just the ability to enrich uranium, but also the missile technology needed to develop a nuclear weapon.

"Today, Iran has the ability to enrich uranium to weapons grade and to produce missiles that could carry a nuclear weapon. Iran wants ultimately to have missiles that could reach the United States and eventually Iran will possess that capability as well."

Would a nuclear-armed Iran be a threat to the continued existence of Israel?

"For us, a nuclear-armed Iran is an existential threat," he stressed. "We live here and we want to live here. We have to be ready to defend our citizens and our country."

From Yaalon's point of view, Iran's achieving a nuclear weapons capability is a game changer in the Middle East that Israel cannot afford to tolerate.

My Research for *Why Israel Can't Wait*

To prepare for writing this book, I spent three weeks in Israel, from May 26, 2009, to June 16. During that time, I conducted numerous interviews with top Israeli government officials, members of the Knesset, two former heads of the Mossad, Israel's intelligence agency, as well as several high-ranking officers from Israeli Defense Forces intelligence. I also interviewed several think-tank leaders and Israeli journalists who specialize in Iran. I was introduced to Prime Minister Netanyahu and had a short one-on-one meeting with President Peres. I traveled extensively in Israel to see firsthand strategically important areas, including the Golan Heights, the Gaza Strip, and the West Bank.

This was a historic time to be in Israel: On Thursday, June 4, President Obama spoke in Cairo, Egypt; on Friday, June 5, President Obama visited the former Buchenwald concentration camp in Germany. On Sunday, June 7, Lebanon held parliamentary elections, with Hezbollah vying to control the legislature. On Friday, June 12, Iran held presidential elections, after which Ayatollah Khamenei declared incumbent president Mahmoud Ahmadinejad the victor, despite claims by the regime of widespread voter fraud. On Sunday, June 14, Prime Minister Benjamin Netanyahu responded to President Obama with a speech televised in Israel.

I had been in Israel many times before. This time I returned there because I perceived the time for dealing with a nuclear-armed Iran is growing short. I wanted to determine how Iran was being perceived by Israel's top government policy makers.

I also wanted to understand from Israel's point of view how the Obama administration's Middle Eastern policies and support for Israel were being judged.

The decision to publish this book now reflects the urgency with which the Iranian nuclear question is coming upon the world. Very likely, 2009 will be "The Year of Iran," whether we like it or not.

If Iran's nuclear program continues through the end of 2009, we will have another "Year of Iran" in 2010. Iran and Israel will dominate the news and U.S. foreign policy until the issue of Iran's nuclear weapons program is resolved, one way or the other.

This is my third book on Iran; I previously published *Atomic Iran*[2] in 2005 and, with Michael Evans, *Showdown with Nuclear Iran*[3] in 2006.

In 2005, I participated in the Iran Freedom Walk. I walked over two hundred miles, from the Liberty Bell in Philadelphia to the White House in Washington, with a group of Iranian expatriates who were determined to restore freedom to their country. We broadcast into Iran via the television and radio stations located in the United States and operated by other Iranian expatriates dedicated to bringing a message of freedom and hope to their homeland.

As a senior staff reporter for World Net Daily, I continue to follow and report on Iran on a constant basis.

Aaron Klein, World Net Daily's Israel-based correspondent and a trusted colleague, assisted me in Israel and was gracious enough to serve as my guide as we toured sensitive areas of the country, such as the Golan Heights. Klein has become known for his ability to interview admitted terrorists, and he has direct access to key operatives in Hamas and the Palestinian Authority.

My Purpose in Writing This Book

I have always believed a war with Iran is the worst possible solution to stopping Iran from developing a nuclear weapons program. I have always favored peaceful change from within, in which a popular uprising such as the world witnessed in Iran after the 2009 presidential election would develop into regime change, by which Iran's totalitarian government, dominated by Shiite religious extremists, could be overthrown. Unfortunately, Iran's brutal suppression of the postelection protests following the June 2009 presidential election removes any hope that regime change is likely to occur in Iran in the foreseeable future.

My prediction today is the same as the one I made dating back to 2004, when I began writing *Atomic Iran*: direct negotiations with Iran are doomed to failure, largely because of the Iranian regime's messianic and apocalyptic revolutionary religious zeal, which the United States and the West in general have tended to underestimate. In addition, the West lacks resolve to apply the extremely rigorous and severe economic and diplomatic sanctions against Iran that have in the past been successfully applied to nations such as South Africa during apartheid. Moreover, Russia and China have remained economically and diplomatically close to Iran despite the UN sanctions, with China investing heavily in Iran to obtain access to Iran's abundant oil and natural-gas reserves.

Iran funds and arms Hezbollah in Lebanon and Hamas in the Gaza, two terrorist organizations that even today remain dedicated to the destruction of Israel. Iran remains a principal terror master in the world and a continuing cause of disorder in the Middle East. Now, with Iran's nuclear weapons program proceeding undeterred, Iran is rapidly becoming an imminent threat to the survival of Israel, potentially greater than any that Israel has ever before faced.

When I was in Israel, there was considerable discussion among the top Israeli government leaders about whether it was wise to meet with me. As author of *The Obama Nation*, I am widely known as the leading critical biographer of President Obama. The Israeli government realizes the sensitivity of trying to work successfully with the Obama administration, especially after President Obama has made abundantly clear the administration's intent to stop all Israeli developments in the West Bank and to demand a two-state solution be implemented immediately, regardless of the stated intent of Hamas to destroy Israel.

The Israeli government also recognizes me as the author

of *Atomic Iran* and understands the degree to which I, a Roman Catholic from birth, have supported the Jewish State of Israel since I was old enough to remember. My concern that Israel survive stems not from evangelical beliefs, but from my conviction as a child that when President Truman allowed the United Nations to partition Palestine in 1948, he correctly understood himself to be making a decision of biblical proportions.

In the final analysis, the government of Israel made a decision during my three-week visit: the State of Israel had something to communicate to the world, and the leaders of Israel decided I would be an acceptable if not appropriate messenger.

The message is simple: *Israel will not attack Iran unless Israel feels abandoned by the world at the moment Iran is about to have nuclear weapons capability.* Before attacking Iran, Israel will plead with the West and the moderate Islamic world to help disarm Iran's nuclear weapons capability in a meaningful manner.

However, the Jewish State of Israel reserves the right of self-defense and will exercise that right, with or without the prior approval of the United States of America.

ONE

Postelection Turmoil in Iran

Following the June 12, 2009, election in Iran, the world was hit by citizen-produced videos and still photographs showing millions of Iranians in the street peacefully protesting what was perceived as a fraudulent declaration by Ayatollah Khamenei that President Mahmoud Ahmadinejad had won a second term as president.

While the Iranian government moved to shut down foreign press reports documenting the postelection protest, Internet websites such as Facebook, YouTube, and especially Twitter came of age. Citizen journalists armed with cell phones, cameras, and camcorders captured images that were broadcast around the world, filling in the gap in professionally produced news. The immediacy of these obviously amateur images generated in the heat of the moment captured powerfully the emotions of millions of Iranians who dared to assemble in street protests and march under the green banners that had come to symbolize their anger. Green was the color of presidential candidate Mir-Hossein Mousavi, the former Iranian prime minister, who, protestors presumed, had won it in a landslide only to see the election stolen from him by the old line of religious clerics who control Iran's governing Guardian Council.

Regime Moves to Crush Postelection Protest

On June 19, Iran's Supreme Leader Ayatollah Ali Hoseyni Khamenei made a rare speech at the Friday prayer service at Tehran University to declare that Ahmadinejad had achieved "absolute victory" and to threaten that those who "ignore or break the law" by continued protests would face the consequences, including being held accountable "for all the violence, bloodshed and rioting."[4] From this moment on, the Iranian regime had spoken, crushing Mousavi's hope for a new vote and putting all Iranian citizens on notice that the riot police and Basij would no longer hesitate to use violence to put down any and all expressions of dissent. The Basij are Iran's brutal civilian vigilante force, estimated to number in the millions and best understood as a group of thugs ready to enforce the regime's dictates.

Almost immediately after Khamenei spoke, the regime sent out hundreds of fully armed riot police on motorcycles and thousands of Basij to crush the protests. The Basij entered the fray armed with batons and pipes that could be used to beat protestors and inflict massive vandalism, especially upon the student dorms at Tehran University, which the Basij promptly invaded and left in shambles.

What emerged over the next ten days were images that resembled the "police riots" in the civil rights and antiwar protests of the 1960s in the United States. These photos and videos had even more impact because of their impromptu nature. The beatings of protestors, the tear gas, the shootings, and the vandalism of the Basij all conveyed an emotional impact beyond any professionally generated news video, especially with the frightened or outraged comments of the photographers being heard in Farsi over the screams and shouts of the dispersed protestors, all punctuated by the crack of gunfire. The nightly citizen-generated videos sent via the Internet from Iran showed rooftop shouts in the Tehran darkness exclaiming "Allahu Akbar," the same "Allah is great" chant that Ayatollah Khomeini–inspired revolutionaries used in 1979 to overthrow the shah.

The Green Sea Marches

With some 70 percent of Iran's population under the age of thirty, the pent-up frustration with a repressive regime that punishes even the slightest moral digression from Islamic law threatened to boil over into revolution, not simply a demand for a fair election. The "green sea" of millions that took to the streets to protest Mousavi's defeat threatened to become like the Ukrainian "orange revolution," in which millions of people in the street were all that was needed to overthrow a totalitarian regime the people no longer cared to tolerate.

Prior to the June 12 election, Iran expert Michael Ledeen of the Foundation for the Defense of Democracies claimed Mousavi was not a revolutionary but rather "a leader who has been made into a revolutionary by a movement that grew up around him."[5]

Mousavi is best known for the role he played as prime minister of Iran from 1981 to 1989 in directing Iran's disastrous eight-year war against Iraq. During that war, millions of Iranians died in near-suicidal battles. Thousands of Iranian children lost their lives being sent first into battle to clear minefields in suicidal attacks with little keys around their necks to remind them they would be in heaven that day. Mousavi was Iran's prime minister on October 23, 1983, when a truck driven by Hezbollah suicide bombers attacked the U.S. Marine Corps barracks in Beirut, Lebanon, killing 241 American troops.[6] Granted, in retirement Mousavi returned to his profession as an architect, while he perfected his skills as an amateur artist and would-be poet. But the impression in the United States that Mousavi was a reformist is entirely wrong.

The real revolutionary, Ledeen claimed, is Mousavi's wife, Zahra Rahnavard, and the real question is why Ayatollah Khamenei allowed her to be positioned that way in the 2009 presidential election.

President Obama Reacts

Under increasing pressure to support the protestors openly, President Obama commented that the world was "watching" the Iranian protests, a mild statement of rebuke to Khamenei's thinly veiled threat to use violence to stop street demonstrations.

The contrast with President Reagan was stark. In 1981, when the Polish government imposed martial law to suppress the Solidarity uprising that had started in Gdansk, President Reagan told a press conference, "We view the current situation in Poland in the gravest of terms, particularly the increasing use of force against an unarmed population and the violations of the basic civil rights of the Polish people."[7] Reagan is also remembered for directly challenging the former Soviet Union in his speech at the Brandenburg Gate in Berlin on June 12, 1987, when he taunted, "Mr. Gorbachev, tear down this wall!"

The theme that the United States would stand for freedom worldwide was articulated by President John F. Kennedy, when he said famously in his 1961 inaugural address, "Let every nation know, whether it wishes us well or ill, that we shall pay any price, bear any burden, meet any hardship, support any friend, oppose any foe, in order to assure the survival and the success of liberty." The theme was continued when President George W. Bush proclaimed in his second inaugural address, "When you stand for liberty, we will stand with you." President Obama himself in his historic speech in Cairo on June 4, only eight days before the contested Iranian election, included "the freedom to live as you choose" when he declared, "These are not just American ideas; they are human rights. And that is why we will support them everywhere."[8]

In Cairo, President Obama presented himself as the leader of the free world. Days later, challenged with the Iranian uprising in the streets, President Obama hesitated to offend the oppressive regime.

In sharp contrast, the House of Representatives passed, 405 to 1, a strongly worded nonbinding resolution expressing support "for all Iranian citizens who embrace the values of freedom, human rights, civil liberties, and the rule of law." The Senate quickly joined the House in passing the Iran resolution by a voice vote. Recalling the fundamental freedoms articulated in documents such as the Declaration of Independence, Senator John McCain took strong exception to President Obama's reluctance to intervene directly in the Iran protests. McCain told Fox News anchor Neil Cavuto that if he had been elected president, "I would say, 'We support the rights of all human beings, especially those in Iran who want to peacefully protest and disagree with their government. We support those fundamental, inalienable rights.'"[9]

Neda's Death, an Iranian Icon for Revolutionary Change

As the street violence escalated in Tehran, one video in particular became haunting. Though less than a minute long, the video was horrifying, as it showed a young woman dying on the street after being shot through her heart by a bullet from an unseen police officer or Basij. Neda, whose name in Farsi means "voice" or "calling," died with her arms outstretched above her head and her eyes fixed open, as if staring into the camera, as blood began surging from her mouth and nose, while those who came to her aid pleaded hysterically for her not to die and bystanders in shock tried in vain to revive her. "Don't be afraid, don't be afraid, don't be afraid, Neda dear, don't be afraid," a white-haired man in a striped blue and white shirt is heard repeating in Farsi throughout a longer version of the video, his voice escalating in shock as he realizes Neda is quickly slipping away.[10] The man was later identified as Neda's professor; additional videos surfaced showing Neda walking calmly with him among the protestors only moments before she was shot to death.

As soon as the video was posted on the Internet, the image of Neda dying was seen worldwide. It became iconic, coming to symbolize the pain Iranian citizens felt protesting in the streets for their freedom against a brutal regime determined to suppress the protests at all costs. Acknowledging the impact of the video to generate outrage, the regime barred Neda's family from holding a public funeral. Lara Setrakian of ABC News communicated via Twitter that the Basij forcefully dispersed a memorial of some one to two thousand people who gathered in 7 Tir Square for Neda.[11] By Monday, June 22, 2009, the riot police and Basij were out in Tehran in force, willing to violently attack and break up any small gatherings of people in the streets to prevent them from grouping together into a protest mass. With the populace disarmed, the regime's strategy to use massive force was bound to succeed, once protestors realized that their continued gathering in the street risked their being beaten, arrested, and possibly even shot by fully armed riot police and baton-wielding Basij.

Through the chaos, the Guardian Council admitted that in fifty Iranian cities the number of votes cast in the presidential election exceeded the number of eligible voters, providing a clear sign the election had been fraudulent, as Mousavi had claimed.[12] Still, Ayatollah Khamenei showed no signs of backing down, as the protest violence threatened to become not just a call for a new election but a threat to the survival of the regime itself. Meanwhile, the Basij began posting on its website images of the citizen videos of protests, with individual protestors being hunted for arrest by isolating them from the crowds with red circles placed around their faces like targets.[13] The Basij were asking Iranians loyal to the regime to turn in their fellow citizens identified as traitors for their in-street protests in which they challenged the legitimacy of the election and the authority of the Supreme Leader to declare the victor.

Hundreds of protestors were arrested, with reports circulating on Twitter from Iran charging that the Basij were going into hospitals to arrest injured protestors, and being stationed outside foreign embassies to arrest anyone seeking to enter for asylum or medical assistance.

An End to Direct Negotiations?

The postelection chaos was clearly not in the White House script, in which candidate Obama had announced during the 2008 presidential election campaign that if elected president, he intended to enter direct negotiations with the Iranian regime without preconditions.[14]

After the regime exercised violence to put down the postelection protests, it came to light that before the elections President Obama had sent a then-undisclosed letter to Ayatollah Khamenei, calling for an improvement in relations and offering once again to engage in direct negotiations. The *Washington Times* broke the story by disclosing that Khamenei confirmed the letter at the end of his sermon at the June 19 Friday prayer service in Tehran.[15] The *Washington Times* reported that the letter was sent between May 4 and May 10 and laid out the prospect of "cooperation in regional and bilateral relations," with the additional prospect of a resolution of the dispute over Iran's nuclear program.

As the crisis evolved, President Obama continued to chart a cautious response in the concern that if the White House supported the protestors openly and strongly, the Iranian regime might blame the dissent upon the United States and the CIA. In an exclusive interview with CBS *Early Show* co-anchor Harry Smith, President Obama responded to critics charging he had not spoken out strongly enough in support of the street protestors and freedom in Iran: "The last thing I want to do," President Obama said, "is to have the United States be a foil for those forces inside Iran who would love nothing better than to make this an argument about the United States."[16] What the White House risked was that President Obama would be blamed if the Iranian regime managed to suppress violently the protestors in Iran. President Obama was trying to hedge his bets by not opposing loudly an Ahmadinejad government he intended later to engage in direct talks.

The administration also expressed concerns that the Iranian regime would have an excuse to suppress protestors even more brutally if White House condemnations of the regime could be interpreted as U.S. instigations of civil disobedience or even rebellion in Iran. Yet, as the Khamenei-Ahmadinejad regime moved to take violent steps to oppress the opposition, the White House position rapidly became undermined. Despite President Obama's measured response to the post-election protests, Iran still blamed the United States for "intolerable" interference in its domestic affairs.[17]

As the Iranian regime's willingness to suppress its own people became apparent, the question could not be avoided: *How could the White House enter into negotiations with an Iranian regime that cared nothing about the freedom and self-determination of its own citizens?* On a practical level, the brutal response of the Iranian security forces to gain control of a population in protest undermined Obama administration expectations of gaining concessions on continued uranium enrichment and the aggressive development of nuclear weapons.

In suppressing the protest, Khamenei moved even further to the political right, supporting incumbent president Ahmadinejad's reelection and moving quickly to stonewall any serious investigation into whether the election results had been manipulated by the regime itself. By declaring Ahmadinejad's victory, Khamenei implicitly affirmed that Ahmadinejad's policies, including Iran's nuclear weapons policy, had been Khamenei's policies all along.

On a moral level, by entering into direct negotiations with the Khamenei-Ahmadinejad regime without preconditions, President Obama will now risk being seen as conveying legitimacy to a corrupt regime opposed by millions of its own citizens. If direct talks are now to occur, millions who followed the Iranian protests on the Internet and protested in the streets of their own countries to support the "green-sea marches" will be immediately disillusioned to see President Obama abandon hope for change in Iran in such a calculated fashion.

As the street protestors in Iran were suppressed by massive force, it became increasingly hard to imagine how President Obama could politically survive the image of him shaking hands with President Ahmadinejad in direct negotiations. Or, as poster "Jahanazad" asked on Twitter: "A question to Obama: Do you really want to sit down at table with a man whose hands are soaked in ppl's [people's] blood?"

In the final analysis, despite the regime's brutal suppression of the postelection dissent, the Internet images made clear that Iran had changed internally. "Even if you can't identify a real political power that might be able to challenge the Iranian regime, the energy is there," Israel's Vice Prime Minister Yaalon stressed in our interview in Jerusalem two days after the Iranian election. "The regime will arrest people and execute people, as well as shut down the Internet capacity—they will close Facebook and Twitter, but the energy is there and the West should play a role in encouraging this energy to be directed toward internal change." Yaalon further qualified that toppling the Iranian regime was not even necessary: "The regime is too brutal, and it might be counterproductive to oppose the regime directly with the goal of toppling the regime. It should be done in a smarter way, one in which the external pressure will serve the people's need to have an internal political change."

What remained in doubt was whether or not President Obama would be able to rise to the occasion to play a meaningful role in the regime change the green-sea marches offered as a political prospect.

At his June 23 press conference, President Obama stepped up the rhetoric, saying he was "appalled and outraged" by the threats and confrontations from the Iranian government in the streets of Tehran. Still, he stopped short of condemning directly the Iranian regime, and he declined to say direct talks with the Iranian regime were now off the table.[18]

Still, the question remained: *How could President Obama possibly expect to make progress sitting down with an Iranian regime that after violently suppressing the postelection protests had become more dangerous than ever?*

TWO

Iran's Nuclear Weapons Program

What proof is there that Iran is pursuing a nuclear weapons program?

IAEA Evidence

On June 17, 2009, the BBC reported that the director of the International Atomic Energy Agency (IAEA), Mohammed ElBaradei, in an interview with the BBC's Middle East editor Jeremy Bowen, said, "It is my gut feeling that Iran would like to have the technology to enable it to have nuclear weapons, if it decides to do so."[19]

This was the first time ElBaradei had gone so far as to deny that the sole purpose of Iran's nuclear program was for the peaceful purposes of generating electricity.

"They [the Iranians] want to send a message to their neighbors, to the rest of the world, don't mess with us," ElBaradei continued. "But the ultimate aim of Iran, as I understand it, is that they want to be recognized as a major power in the Middle East."

"This is to them the road to get that recognition, to get that power and prestige," the IAEA head continued. "It is also an insurance policy against what they have heard in the past about regime change."

The BBC also reported that Ali Asghar Soltanieh, Iran's ambassador to the IAEA, said ElBaradei was "absolutely wrong."

"We don't have any intention of having nuclear weapons at all," Soltanieh told reporters. "But we are going to have nuclear technology for peaceful purposes. We will continue fuel-cycle activities without any interruption because Iran has a legitimate need."

Iran has used the IAEA's term *fuel cycle* as code language justifying Iran's right as a signatory of the Nuclear Non-Proliferation Treaty to develop nuclear fuel for peaceful purposes. Since the latter Bush administration, Iran has rejected UN- and IAEA-supported offers from Russia to enrich uranium for peaceful purposes. Instead, Iran has insisted upon the right to enrich uranium in Iran under Iranian direction and management as part of the nation's right to the "full fuel cycle."

2007 U.S. National Intelligence Estimate

In November 2007, the combined intelligence agencies of the United States issued a surprising National Intelligence Estimate that reported with "high confidence" that Iran stopped its nuclear weapons program in the fall of 2003.[20] Nonetheless, a statement by ElBaradei published on the IAEA website on June 15, 2009, suggested Iran has resumed its nuclear weapons program since that date. "Although sixteen U.S. intelligence agencies said Iran stopped alleged work on nuclear studies in 2003, we do not know whether it has stopped or not," ElBaradei said. "We continue to receive new information. We also do not know whether the information is authentic or not."[21]

Israeli intelligence is also convinced that Iran stopped its nuclear weapons program in the fall of 2003 and that Iran resumed the weapons program shortly after that time. Two former Mossad heads confirmed this point in private interviews held in Israel in June 2009. Danny Yaton, director general of Mossad from 1996 to 1998 and chief of staff for Prime Minister Ehud Barak from 1991 to 2001, unequivocally asserted that Iran is currently pursuing a nuclear weapons program.[22] Shabtai Shavit, director general of Mossad from 1989 to 1996, agreed. Shavit attributed Iran's temporary cessation of the nuclear program to *hudna*, a word in Arabic that means "truce" or "armistice." The concept, Shavit explained, was that *hudna* is considered a tactical cessation of hostilities that Islamic law authorizes in times of stress, such that the continuing world struggle can be resumed more aggressively once circumstances return to being more favorable. "When Iran realized the United States was willing to send 150,000 troops to Iraq, Iran was frightened the U.S. would not hesitate to go on to Iran," Shavit explained. "This decision was based on the concept of 'hudna.'"[23]

General Yaalon also agreed. "If we have to look back to what is the best strategy to deal with Iran today, there was a precedent and we have to look back to 2003," Yaalon told the author. "Then Ayatollah Khamenei decided to suspend Iran's nuclear weapons operation for a while." When questioned directly on this issue, Yaalon insisted a second time that Israeli intelligence supported the conclusion that Iran did stop its nuclear program "for a while" in 2003. "The U.S. National Intelligence Estimate was correct in that Iran stopped the nuclear program in 2003, but the NIE neglected to mention that by 2006, Iran renewed their nuclear weapons program at a higher level." Why did Iran suspend the program? "Because in 2003, the American strategy of the Bush administration after 9/11 was an offensive strategy of preemption," he explained.

"Phase One was Afghanistan and Phase Two was Iraq," he continued. "The main question among rogue leaders in the region was this: 'Who might be next?' At that point Libya's Muammar Qaddafi decided to give up his nuclear project. And at that point Iran's Ayatollah Khamenei decided not to give any excuse to President Bush to attack."

This, to Yaalon, made an important point that Iran was susceptible to international pressure, as long as the international pressure included a credible threat that Iran would suffer serious harm if it refused to comply.

"So, for those who claim the military option is not an

option, there is no way to discuss any issue with the Iranian regime or with any other extremist in the region without having a credible military option as a very big stick," he stressed. "You might achieve the same effect by economic sanctions of sufficient magnitude that the Iranian regime would be threatened with economic collapse. But there is no way to convince Iran to stop their nuclear weapons program without a very big stick."

Iran Advances All Components of a Nuclear Weapons Program

A credible nuclear program must have three components:

1. A source of weapons-grade enriched uranium or plutonium;

2. A medium- or long-range missile system capable of delivering a nuclear weapons payload reliably; and

3. The technology to weaponize the weapons-grade enriched uranium or plutonium into a miniaturized warhead capable of being delivered by a medium- or long-range missile.

Since 2006, Iran has made progress on all three components.

On February 19, 2009, the *New York Times* reported that
IAEA inspectors had discovered an additional 460 pounds
of low-enriched uranium, a third more than Iran had previously disclosed. The *Times* further reported that Iran had
amassed more than a ton of low-enriched uranium, enough
with added purification to make at least one atomic bomb.[24]
Then, on June 5, 2009, the *Times* reported that Iran had
increased its number of installed centrifuges to 7,200, more
than enough to make fuel for up to two weapons a year, if
the Iranian government decided to use its facilities for that
purpose.[25]

On May 20, 2009, the Associated Press reported that Iran
had successfully test-fired a missile that could hit Israel.[26]
Iran's solid-fuel Sajjil-2 surface-to-surface missile has a range
of 1,200 miles, according to the AP. A solid-fuel missile has
two strategic military advantages:

1. Solid-fuel missiles can be fired immediately,
   reducing the time antimissile systems have to detect
   a launch; and

2. Solid-fuel missiles tend to be more accurate than
   liquid-fuel missiles of similar range.

"Defense Minister [Mostafa Mohammad Najjar] has
informed me that the Sajjil-2 missile, which has very ad-
vanced technology, was launched from Semnan and it landed

precisely on target," the AP quoted Iran's President Ahmadinejad as saying on state radio. The Sajjil-2 missile is a significant improvement over the Shahab-3 medium-range ballistic missile Iran has had in its arsenal since at least 2004.[27]

The IAEA has charged that Iran is not cooperating with its requests for an answer to questions about possible studies on nuclear warheads Iran has carried out in the past, according to a report published by the BBC in May 2009.[28] A May 2009 Senate Foreign Relations Committee report titled "Iran: Where We Are Today," issued by the committee's Democratic chairman, Senator John Kerry, reported: "Potentially damning evidence surfaced in 2004 when U.S. intelligence obtained a laptop computer from an Iranian engineer."[29] The Senate report said the computer contained "thousands of pages of data on tests of high explosives and designs for a missile capable of carrying a nuclear warhead. It also contained videos of what were described as secret workshops around Iran where the weapons work was supposedly carried out."

The Senate report also pointed out that the Iranians denounced these computer documents as fakes. Still, senior UN officials and intelligence officers who saw these documents told the committee staff that "the documents come from more than just the laptop and appear to be authentic, right down to the names, addresses and telephone numbers of the workshops in Iran."

The Senate committee concluded that "Iran has moved closer to completing the three components for a nuclear weapon—fissile material, warhead design and delivery system."[30]

President Obama's Assessment

President Obama has left no doubt that the White House has concluded Iran is pursuing nuclear weapons.

On November 7, 2008, in his first press conference after winning the presidential election, President-elect Obama said, "Iran's development of a nuclear weapon, I believe, is unacceptable. And we have to mount an international effort to prevent that from happening."[31]

In the press availability following President Obama's meeting with Israeli prime minister Benjamin Netanyahu on May 18, 2009, Obama said, "I indicated to Prime Minister Netanyahu in private what I have said publicly, which is that Iran obtaining a nuclear weapon would not only be a threat to Israel and a threat to the United States, but would be profoundly destabilizing in the international community as a whole and could set off a nuclear-arms race in the Middle East that would be extraordinarily dangerous for all concerned, including for Iran."[32]

But what precisely were President Obama and Prime Minister Netanyahu envisioning?

THREE

Hezbollah, Hamas, and Syria

In 2006, Israel fought a war against Hezbollah in Lebanon, one known in Israel as the Second Lebanon War. Beginning at the end of December 2008, Israel fought a war against Hamas in the Gaza, code-named by Israel "Operation Cast Lead." In the immediate aftermath of both wars, Iran moved to rearm both Hezbollah and Hamas with more rockets than either had possessed prior to the hostilities.

Both Hezbollah and Hamas function as surrogate terrorist organizations that operate under directions from Tehran; both Hezbollah and Hamas remain sworn to the destruction of the Jewish State of Israel.

"From the military perspective, not a lot has changed since [Iran's June 12 presidential election]," Admiral Michael Mullen, chairman of the U.S. Joint Chiefs of Staff, told Fox News in an interview broadcast on June 27, 2009. "The Iranians are still proliferators in terms of terrorism, in terms of their ideology. They still support Hezbollah and Hamas. [The

Iranians] have been a destabilizing influence and they continue on a path to develop nuclear weapons."

Military intelligence in Israel shares the assessment of the
U.S. military regarding Iran's grip on Hezbollah and Hamas.

Hezbollah, an Iranian Surrogate

"Hezbollah is an organization which was created by Iran,"
Major General (res.) Yaakov Amidror told the author in an
interview. "Given my background in the military and in government, I know the relationship between Hezbollah and
Iran not only from the headquarters, but also from the situation on the ground."

Amidror headed the research and assessment division of
Israeli defense intelligence from 1992 through 1996. He then
served as the military secretary to Israel's ministry of defense
from 1996 to 1998. Following that he was the commander
of the Israeli National Defense College. Amidror currently
serves as the director of the Institute for Contemporary Affairs at the Jerusalem Center for Public Affairs.

Hezbollah traces its roots to Najaf in Iraq. Najaf is an
important Shiite center of theology where Ayatollah Muhammad Hussein Fadlallah, the spiritual leader of Hezbollah,
studied when he was in exile from Lebanon; there Fadlallah
met Ayatollah Khomeini, who himself was in exile from Iran.
Hezbollah as an organization arose in 1982, given birth by
the disorder in the Lebanese Shiite community caused by

the 1982 war in which Israel invaded and occupied southern Lebanon.

Amidror explained that the current secretary general of Hezbollah, Hassan Nasrallah, is also the personal representative of the Supreme Leader of Iran.

"Nasrallah is not an Iranian ambassador, because Iran has an ambassador to Lebanon," Amidror said. "But Nasrallah is there to represent Ayatollah Khamenei, the Supreme Leader of Iran. It means that Nasrallah has a direct link with the highest decision makers in Iran, not through the mechanism of the Iranian Revolutionary Guards Corps or the al-Quds [Jerusalem] Forces as they are called in Iran, but directly between the secretary general of Hezbollah as a person and the Supreme Leader of Iran as a person."

Amidror discredited any notion that Hezbollah had moderated as a result of becoming a political party operating within the government of Lebanon.

"Many Israelis believe that because Hezbollah has become stronger politically, at the end of the day, it will be moderated by the responsibility of being part of the system," he said. "Many Israelis will have to learn in the hard way that just as most of the extremist movements in the Islamic world, Hezbollah is not becoming more moderate. Look at Al Qaeda, look at the mullahs in Iran, Hassan al-Turabi in Sudan, and Hamas in the Gaza—they are all extremists, and the same is true about Hezbollah.

"The belief in many places that by gaining control and

responsibility, those movements will compromise part of their principles is a huge mistake. What these groups have in mind is that they have succeeded only because they have fulfilled their obligations to their ideology—and to God, if you want—and this is why they continue to be the same extremists they were before they participated in elections and government.

"The strongest point of Hezbollah is that they have the backing of Iran," he continued. "Hezbollah has the money, the experts, and the know-how from Iran."

"Some ninety percent of the rockets coming to Hezbollah in Lebanon have come from Iran through Syria," Amidror stressed. "The rockets arrive at the Damascus International Airport by airplane from Iran. From there, the Iranian rockets are driven by truck convoys escorted by Syrian military authorities into Lebanon through the Bekaa Valley.

"Without Iran's money there would be no Hezbollah in Lebanon," he emphasized. "Without Iran's money, Hezbollah would be a strictly Lebanese organization and it would be one of many. Iran provides Hezbollah the money Hezbollah needs to operate, the weapons and the training. You cannot make any fine line of distinction between Hezbollah and Iran. At the end of the day, Hezbollah is an extension of Iran in Lebanon.

"Since the 2006 war, Iran has more than fully resupplied Hezbollah with rockets," he concluded. "Make no mistake about it: the source of instability in the Middle East today is Iran."

Dr. Reuven Erlich, director of the Intelligence and Terrorism Information Center at the Center for Special Studies in Israel, agreed with Major General Amidror's assessment of the risk presented by Hezbollah and Iran. Erlich served in the IDF Intelligence Corps, mainly as an analyst specializing in Syrian, Lebanese, and Palestinian affairs. He retired from the IDF in 1994 with the rank of colonel after thirty years of service in staff and operational duties.[33]

"Hezbollah is a pure Iranian proxy," Erlich explained in an interview from his Tel Aviv office. "Hezbollah's strategy and ideology come from Iran. The Iranian Revolutionary Guard established Hezbollah from the beginning, going back to the 1980s, even though the Revolutionary Guard today keeps a low profile in Lebanon."[34]

"Iran permanently supplies Hezbollah with rockets and other weapons, from before the Second Lebanon War in 2006, until today, on a continual basis," he said. "You cannot supply a military force on the scale of Hezbollah only by smuggling arms."

Erlich agreed with Amidror that most of the Iranian weapons reach Hezbollah through Syria via the Bekaa Valley. He stressed that Hezbollah military operatives are sent to Iran for military training on a continual basis.

The website of the Intelligence and Terrorism Information Center displays many Iranian documents prepared for Hezbollah that were confiscated in 2006 during the Second Lebanon War.[35] The documents prominently display Iranian

Supreme Leader Ali Khamenei and the instigator of the Islamic revolution, Ayatollah Khomeini, instead of Lebanese heroes. To export the Iranian revolution to Lebanon, together Iran and Hezbollah operate an extensive network of religious, educational, cultural, and social institutions as well as publishing houses. The network is used "to inculcate Lebanese society, primarily the Shi'ite community, with Iranian radical Islamic ideology."

Hezbollah's publications in Lebanon include Iranian literature in Arabic translation, with the goal of spreading Iranian ideology in Lebanon and nurturing the personality cult of Ayatollahs Khomeini and Khamenei. As the center describes the collection, the publications inspire hatred against Israel, the United States, and the West in general, encouraging terrorism and violence against Israel, while commemorating Hezbollah's "shahid martyrs" as role models for Lebanese teenagers to become the next generation of Hezbollah military operatives.

Hamas in Gaza Becomes a Second Iranian Terrorist Surrogate

Unlike Hezbollah, Hamas is a Sunni organization controlled by the Palestinians. Even though Hamas is Sunni, while the Iranian leadership is Shiite, Iran supports Hamas on the theory that "the enemy of my enemy is my friend." Hamas owes its origin to the Muslim Brotherhood, a group formed in Egypt in the 1920s with the goal of establishing a "pure" Islamic state. Hamas was officially formed on December 8, 1987, coinciding with the outbreak of the first intifada against Israel. Hamas is an Islamic jihadist organization that operates primarily in the Gaza Strip and other Palestinian-controlled territories. The Egyptian government sees both the Muslim Brotherhood and Hamas as potential threats to the political stability of Egypt itself.

In January 2006, Hamas won a surprise victory in the Palestinian parliamentary elections. The Hamas triumph challenged Mahmoud Abbas, the chairman of the Palestinian Liberation Organization and head of the Fatah Party, for leadership in the Palestinian Authority.[36] Once Hamas gained control of the Palestinian parliament, Shiite Iran moved openly to support Sunni Hamas in common cause against Israel, a decision Iran made choosing to ignore for the time being the obvious religious differences between itself and Hamas. Immediately after Hamas won the legislative elections in January 2006, the United States, the European Union, and Israel blocked aid to Hamas. Then, in an armed conflict culminating in June 2007, Hamas defeated Fatah, thereby weakening the position of Abbas and the PLO in the Palestinian government.

"Abbas has no authority at all in the Gaza," Ali Waked, a freelance correspondent who works with Aaron Klein and World Net Daily, said in an interview with the author in Israel on June 2, 2009. "Fatah cannot even have minimal meetings in Gaza without having the authorization of Hamas. Abbas will never have any influence over the Gaza Strip if Hamas does not agree, unless Israel were to make a strategic decision in the Gaza and insist that Hamas must bring Abbas back into authority in Gaza.

"Hamas charges that since January 9, 2009, Abbas is no longer the legitimate president of the Palestinian Authority since he extended for another year on his own authority his four-year term after it expired," Waked explained. "President Obama wanted to show that for the United States and for the international community Abbas is still the president," he explained, referring to President Obama's meeting with Abbas at the White House on May 28, 2009.[37] "But for the Palestinian people, President Obama meeting with Abbas made no impact at all since they know Abbas is not strong in Gaza and that Abbas in the West Bank is also challenged by Hamas.

"A big change has occurred as the Palestinian people have become more Islamic and under the influence of Iran," he continued. "Even if Hamas were chased from Gaza by Israel, Abbas and Fatah would be surprised to find a more hardline jihadist community that would not welcome them back. Right now, an increasing number of Palestinians agree with Hamas that violent jihad is the only way to get rid of the Israelis. That is today what the young Palestinian people are thinking and believing.

"Iran is moving to control Palestinian society," Waked stressed. "The next step for Iran will be for Hamas to take over the West Bank. Right now, Hamas is infiltrating Fatah organizations in the West Bank with a takeover in mind."

In an important article he wrote before he became vice prime minister, Lieutenant General Moshe Yaalon argued that in the June 2007 armed conflict between Hamas and Fatah, Hamas's violent takeover of Gaza transformed the Strip into the region's first "Islamic Arab Emirate."[38] Yaalon tied Syria directly into the plot, writing, "This was an important achievement for Iran. It is also the region's first example of the Muslim Brotherhood's governmental control of a contiguous territory and population. Iran's direct backing of Hamas via Khaled Meshaal [the head of Hamas in Gaza] and the Damascus-based Hamas leadership has essentially transformed Gaza into a base from which to export Iranian terror against Israel and expand Tehran's political control in the region." Yaalon noted that after Israel's 2005 disengagement from Gaza, Iran has worked tirelessly to transform the Gaza into a de facto Hamas state. The establishment of "Hamastan" in Gaza, Yaalon wrote, "signaled the weakness of the West's political will in confronting and defeating Iran and its proxies."[39]

After Hamas defeated Fatah in 2007, Iran picked up the funding vacuum left when the United States, EU, and Israel refused to continue providing financial support to Hamas. Yaalon noted that in December 2007 alone, some $100 million was smuggled into Gaza by senior Hamas members returning from the hajj pilgrimage to Saudi Arabia. "In

March 2008, Hamas officials admitted for the first time that hundreds of their top operatives have trained in Syria and Iran under the aegis of Iran's Revolutionary Guards Corps (IRGC)," Yaalon wrote. "Hamas officials noted that Iran's training of Hamas is similar to Iran's training of Hezbollah."[40]

Between 2005 and late 2007, some 230 tons of explosives, including scores of antitank and antiaircraft missiles, were smuggled into Gaza via the underground tunnels from the Egyptian Sinai into Gaza. Prior to the 2009 war with Hamas, more than three thousand rockets and mortars were fired at Israel from Gaza by Iranian-sponsored groups, Yaalon noted. Since the Second Lebanon War, Iran has spent more than a billion dollars rebuilding southern Lebanon and bolstering Hezbollah there, he further argued.[41] Israel estimates that Iran has managed to increase Hezbollah's prewar arsenal by almost one-third, such that Hezbollah now possesses as many as sixty thousand rockets, more than three times the rockets Hezbollah had prior to the Second Lebanon War. The longest-range of Hezbollah's rockets in Lebanon, the Iranian-manufactured Zelzal, has a range of between 125 and 156 miles, enough to hit Tel Aviv, Ben-Gurion International Airport, and Jerusalem from southern Lebanon.[42]

The same is true in the Gaza.

"The tunnel operation from Egypt to the Gaza is a huge industry," Waked emphasized. "We are not talking about unique tunnels. Under almost every house in Rafah in the Gaza on the border with Egypt there is a tunnel for smuggling." Rafah is a Palestinian city in the southern Gaza that extends across to the Sinai Peninsula in Egypt.

Hezbollah Admits Supporting Hamas in Gaza

In December 2008, during Operation Cast Lead, Hezbollah secretary general Hassan Nasrallah lashed out against Egypt's President Hosni Mubarak by calling on the Egyptian people and armed forces to compel their leaders to open the Rafah crossing between Gaza and Egypt. The statement amounted to an appeal for popular unrest among the Egyptian people and mutiny in the armed forces, according to a report published by Reuters.[43] Immediately, Egypt lashed back. "You are a man who used to enjoy respect, but you have insulted the Egyptian people," Egyptian foreign minister Ahmed Aboul Gheit said in response, addressing Nasrallah.

Since Hamas defeated Fatah in June 2007, Israel has maintained a strict embargo on Gaza, concerned that open movement of goods into Gaza would allow Hamas easy access to weapons supplied by Iran. Now, after Operation Cast Lead, Hamas is restricted to getting Iranian arms primarily through the remaining tunnel network to Egypt and to some extent by the sea. The Israeli embargo after Operation Cast Lead has blocked reconstruction money from flowing into Gaza primarily because of Israel's concern that international reconstruction funds would result in strengthening Hamas financially and politically, as well as providing a back door through which Hamas in Gaza would be more easily rearmed. Blocked have been more than $5 billion in reconstruction aid pledged to the Gaza by the United States, Saudi Arabia, and several other countries, as well as industrial-level quantities of building materials offered by the UN Relief and Works Agency. While Hamas remains in control of Gaza, Israel has allowed regular shipments of humanitarian aid and commercial goods, including food.[44] Still, Israel has had to counter Hamas-generated propaganda that the Israeli embargo is aimed at blocking humanitarian aid from reaching the Palestinians in Gaza.

Egypt has cooperated with Israel to restrict border access with Gaza, concerned not to encourage the movement of terrorists and weapons into Gaza via Egypt. Egypt is also concerned that open access to Gaza from Egypt would merely serve as a further inducement to Iran to take active steps to politically destabilize Egypt.

In May 2009, Hezbollah openly proclaimed it has been supplying the Palestinians with "every type of support" for some time, in a remarkable admission of Hezbollah's widening regional role, as reported by the *Financial Times* in London.[45] "We have always said that we supported the resistance in Palestine but we have not mentioned how or given details of our support," Hezbollah's Sheikh Naim Qassem told the *Financial Times* from a secret location in southern Beirut. "But Egypt has now revealed that we have given military support to Palestine. We have done so for a while but we have not talked about it." The interview was prompted by an arrest Egypt made the previous month of forty-nine men suspected of being part of a Hezbollah cell planning to attack Egyptian institutions and Israeli tourists. Hezbollah admitted one of the arrested men was a member of Hezbollah but insisted he was on a "logistical mission" related to the Gaza, not on a mission to participate in terrorist attacks in Egypt.

"It is one of the secrets of the resistance that we don't talk about the details of our support, but suffice to say that we are giving them every type of support that could help the Palestinian resistance. Every type that is possible." Pressed by the *Financial Times* to specify if "every possible" type of assistance included Hezbollah providing Hamas training and arms, Qassem said, "We will leave this to be seen in the time to come."

Hezbollah's now-open declaration of support for Hamas provides further evidence for Israel's concern that opening Gaza to international reconstruction and free flow of people and goods from Egypt would only end up arming a very dangerous enemy in control of a virtual Arab emirate within Israel's midst. Hezbollah appears to be working actively to open a "southern front" against Israel in the Egyptian Sinai, in conjunction with Hamas in the Gaza. In any war with Iran, Israel can be certain to receive rocket retaliation from Hezbollah in Lebanon and from Hamas in Gaza, as well as possible military action from Hezbollah operatives in the Sinai.

Syria Unites with Iran to Support Hamas

On June 27, 2009, Syrian officials threatened to take back the Golan Heights by force if a peace agreement with Israel for the return of the strategically valuable plateau is not reached, according to an Israeli Army Radio report published in Israel by *Haaretz*.[46]

A group calling itself the Syrian Committee for the Freedom of Golan has organized among the Druze in the Golan Heights, with the determination to return the Golan Heights to Syria. The Druze in the Golan Heights are a religious offshoot of Islam that combines elements of Islam with Greek philosophy and Gnosticism. *Haaretz* reported that representatives of the Syrian Committee for the Freedom of Golan attended a ceremony along with Syrian president Bashar Assad at a new communications center in Quneitra, a town in the demilitarized United Nations Disengagement Observer Force (UNDOF) Zone between Syria and Israel.

"The communications center will report on the troubles of Syrian residents in the occupied Golan under barbaric and racist Israeli rule," Syrian information minister Mohsen Bilal was quoted as saying at the ceremony, referring to the Druze in the Golan who wish to live under Syrian sovereignty.

In June 2009, the author met and toured the Golan Heights with a Druze member of the Syrian Committee for the Freedom of Golan. His home in the Golan proudly displays pictures of President Assad, and his family enthusiastically proclaims their anticipation of the day when the "occupied Golan" would be liberated from Israel to be returned to Syria.

The author observed several highly sensitive military installations in the Golan Heights with evident technology for listening to and observing Syria that the Israeli Defense Forces have established recently. Also evident were numerous IDF tanks stationed in twenty-four-hour combat readiness among the hills of the Golan Heights, pointed toward Syria.

Israel's negotiations with Syria stopped after Operation Cast Lead, in anticipation of the Israeli elections that ultimately ended the Kadima government of Ehud Olmert to bring to power now–prime minister Benjamin Netanyahu under a coalition headed by the Likud party. Even while the Iranian regime was brutally using force to end the postelection protests in June, the Obama administration announced a decision to reestablish diplomatic relations with Syria by sending a U.S. ambassador to Damascus. Fox News reported, "This diplomatic effort is said by knowledgeable sources to include a quiet campaign by the Obama administration to 'bring Hamas into the process.'"[47]

On May 5, 2009, just a little more than a month before the Iranian presidential elections, Iran's President Ahmadinejad canceled his meeting in Latin America to fly to Damascus instead.[48] Syria's President Assad welcomed Ahmadinejad to Damascus for a series of meetings in what was billed as a state visit from Syria's closest ally in the region. At the conclusion of their meetings, Ahmadinejad told reporters that the relation between Syria and Iran is "deepening and developing on various levels." Assad acknowledged in a joint press conference with Ahmadinejad that the two leaders had discussed the Palestinians, the situation in Iraq, and progress in Iran's nuclear program.

In Damascus, Ahmadinejad also met with Hamas leader Khaled Meshaal and with representatives of nine other Palestinian organizations to send a message to the Netanyahu government that Iran, Syria, and Hamas remained united in their opposition to Israel. "Syria and Iran have been from the very beginning united and in agreement to stand on the side of the Palestinian resistance," Ahmadinejad said. "They will continue to do so. We see [sic] that the resistance will continue until all occupied territories are liberated."[49]

FOUR

President Obama in Cairo

On Thursday, June 4, 2009, President Obama fulfilled a campaign promise by giving a major policy address in a Muslim capital when he spoke at Cairo University in Cairo, Egypt.

Reviewing President Obama's historic fifty-six-minute speech to an audience of some three thousand invited guests in Cairo, the *Jerusalem Post* noted the president was "uncompromising in his demand for the establishment of a Palestinian state, and called for a 'stop to settlements.'"[50]

Clearly, President Obama's intent was to establish a new reconciliation with the Muslim world by reaching out to Islamic moderates. Notably, the president referenced the "Holy Koran" five times and the "Holy Bible" only once. For the vast majority of those listening to the speech in Israel, including top government officials, Obama's Cairo speech marked the beginning of a new relationship with the United States in which U.S. support for Israel could no longer be assumed without qualifications. The speech capped an intensification of pressure on Israel that began almost immediately after the Obama administration took office.

A Two-State Solution

"For decades, then, there has been a stalemate: two peoples with legitimate aspirations, each with a painful history that makes compromise elusive," Obama said, adding that it is "easy to point fingers" when commenting on the Palestinian-Israeli conflict. "The only resolution is for the aspirations of both sides to be met through two states, where Israelis and Palestinians each live in peace and security."[51]

The Netanyahu government, in its first months since taking office in March 2009, had been resistant to proceeding with the "two-state" solution, if the creation of a Palestinian state meant conceding sovereignty to Hamas.

Regarding Hamas, the president noted that "Hamas must put an end to violence, recognize past agreements, [and] recognize Israel's right to exist." President Obama neglected, however, to say what would happen if Hamas refused to fulfill these conditions. Instead he strongly suggested that Israel must end the economic embargo of the Gaza right now, despite the risk that Hamas would use the end of the embargo to rearm more easily. Referring indirectly to the embargo, President Obama said, "Just as it devastates Palestinian families, the continuing humanitarian crisis in Gaza does not serve Israel's security; neither does the continuing lack of opportunity in the West Bank." Again, the president put the burden on Israel: "Progress in the daily lives of the Palestinian people must be a critical part of a road to peace, and Israel must take concrete steps to enable such progress."

In direct contrast to President Obama's demand that Israel end immediately all development in settlements, the president issued no ultimatums to Iran. Instead he appeared to repeat then–secretary of state Madeleine Albright's apology in 2000 for a decades-old incident, the CIA participation in the overthrow of Iranian prime minister Mohammed Mossadegh.

Moreover, the president seemed to sidestep the issue of Iran's nuclear weapons program. "But it is clear to all concerned that when it comes to nuclear weapons, we have reached a decisive point," President Obama commented without calling upon Iran to end immediately its nuclear weapons program. Again, the president almost seemed to apologize to Iran that no demand was being made for Israel to engage in unilateral nuclear disarmament, stating that America was committed "to seek a world in which no nations hold nuclear weapons."

Nor did the president make any reference to Iran's well-documented role in funding and arming Hezbollah and Hamas.

"Natural Growth" Development in Existing Settlements

Regarding settlements, the *Jerusalem Post* noted the day after the speech that the loudest applause President Obama received during his address was when he said, "The United States does not accept the legitimacy of continued Israeli settlements. This construction violates previous agreements and undermines efforts to achieve peace. It is time for these settlements to stop."

Since the middle of May 2009, the Obama administration had telegraphed to Israel that ending all developments in the settlements would be a major objective of the new Middle East foreign policy that President Obama intended to outline in Cairo.

At stake are more than one hundred settlements that Israel has built in the West Bank in the largely Arab East Jerusalem since the 1967 war.[52] "Natural growth" refers to construction in existing settlements designed to meet the needs of growing families. Still, the term is typically not used for the more-contested smaller settlements, where, for instance, a few families build homes or live in trailers without Israeli government authorization.

The Netanyahu government since taking office in March 2009 had also stood firm that natural-growth development in existing government-authorized settlements had been authorized under previous agreements with the United States and would be continued.

In the joint press availability following Prime Minister Netanyahu's first meeting with President Obama in the White House, on May 18, 2009, President Obama pointedly said, "Settlements have to be stopped in order for us to move forward."[53]

Then, in a May 27, 2009, appearance at the State Department with Egyptian foreign minister Ahmed Aboul Gheit, Secretary of State Hillary Clinton made the point unequivocally clear in responding to a question: "With respect to settlements, the President was very clear when Prime Minister Netanyahu was here. He [President Obama] wants to see a stop to settlements—not some settlements, not outposts, not natural-growth exceptions." To make sure the point was driven home, Clinton continued, "We think it is in the best interests of the effort that we are engaged in that settlement expansion cease. That is our position. That is what we have communicated very clearly, not only to the Israelis but to the Palestinians and others. And we intend to press that point."[54]

The Obama administration message that Israel must stop all settlement development continued after the Cairo speech, when special envoy and former Maine Democratic senator George Mitchell visited Israel on June 9, 2009, to hold meetings with top Israeli government officials, including Prime Minister Netanyahu, President Peres, Defense Minister Ehud Barak, and Foreign Minister Avigdor Lieberman.[55]

"Obama's insistence on picking a fight with Israel over settlements rather than prioritizing the menace from Iran is puzzling," Jonathan Tobin, the executive editor of *Commentary* magazine, commented in the *Jerusalem Post*, "since more concessions on settlements are unlikely to advance the peace process with a toothless Palestinian Authority, or its Hamas rivals, neither of which have much interest in accepting a two-state solution that most Israelis already support."[56]

Is Israel's Dispute with the Palestinians a Territorial Dispute?

"Traditionally, most analysts and pundits looking at the Middle East have believed that the source of instability in this region is the unresolved territorial disputes between Israel and its Arab neighbors, most of which they believe emanate from the 1967 Six-Day War," Ambassador Dore Gold told the author in a private interview from his office as president of the Jerusalem Center for Public Affairs.[57] From 1997 to 1999, Gold served as Israel's ambassador to the United Nations. Gold was subsequently a top foreign policy adviser for Prime Minister Ariel Sharon.

"Israel has actually gone through a laboratory test of this thesis in the last few years," he continued. "In 2000, Israel unilaterally withdrew from Lebanon, a country which Israel entered in a war of self-defense in 1982, to uproot the PLO terrorist infrastructure. When Israel pulled out of Lebanon, Israel turned to the United Nations and Secretary-General Kofi Annan actually sent a team to determine that Israel had in fact pulled out of every square inch of Lebanese territory. Then the UN Security Council determined on the basis of Kofi Annan's report that Israel had left Lebanon completely. So there was no political grievance that could have justified any continued Lebanese aggression against Israel."

Still, Hezbollah in Lebanon has continued to launch rockets into Israel, despite Israel's complete withdrawal from all Lebanese territory.

"Then we fast-forward to 2005, when Prime Minister Ariel Sharon decided to unilaterally withdraw the entire Israeli civilian and military presence from the Gaza Strip," he continued. "Israel had a right under UN Security Council Resolution 242 from 1967 to stay in parts of Gaza, claiming Israel was seeking secure, recognized boundaries in the language of the UN resolution. But Israel did not make this claim, because Israel wanted to deny the other side any excuse for continuing the conflict against Israel.

"Israel found that from 2005 onward, it faced increased rocket threats from Hamas in Gaza, as well as from Hezbollah in Lebanon," Gold said. "In fact, the number of rocket attacks that were launched by Hamas from Gaza from 2005 to 2006 increased by a factor of five hundred percent.

"What all this told Israelis was that the source of conflict between Israel and its neighbors and in the region as a whole has nothing to do with the territorial differences between Israel and its neighbors. In both cases of Lebanon and Gaza, territorial differences were resolved, yet war was resumed against Israel."

So what is the source of the conflict?

"What is common to both Lebanon and Gaza is that the main terrorist organizations operating in those areas, Hezbollah in Lebanon and Hamas in Gaza, are supported by Iran," he explained. "Therefore, Israelis perceive that the war being waged against them is not over some territorial grievance any longer, but related to Iran's quest for regional hegemony—the main issue Israel has to deal with today.

"Beyond that, Israel has no doubt Iran is pursuing a nuclear weapons capability," Gold continued. "Israelis, regardless of their political persuasion, do not buy into the argument made in some circles that Iran's nuclear program is limited to civilian purposes. Israelis take seriously that behind Iran's improving capabilities in the nuclear field and with respect to its missiles and delivery-system capabilities, Iran has clear-cut and announced intent to destroy the State of Israel."

Israel's Right to Natural-Growth Development of Settlements

Clearly, the Obama administration's emphasis on stopping all Israeli development of existing settlements indicates that the president continues to think the Israeli-Palestinian conflict remains a dispute over territory.

"The issue of settlements is an overstated subject," Gold responded. "If you take all settlements of the West Bank and you add up how much territory they take up, you are talking about somewhere between 1.7 percent to 5 percent of the total available land.

"So if you are talking about 'natural growth' development when a family has a child, for instance, how much land is expended for that purpose?" he asked. "It is infinitesimal. Nevertheless, the issue has become a big issue in Israeli-U.S. relations so far under the Obama administration.

"When Yasser Arafat negotiated the Oslo Accords under President Clinton in 1993, he thought of putting in a settlement freeze, but then–prime minister Yitzhak Rabin and then–foreign minister Shimon Peres refused. Nonetheless, Arafat had his assistants sign the Oslo Accords, even though there was no settlement freeze inside. In other words, a settlement freeze was not sufficiently important to Arafat to hold up signature on the Oslo Accords in 1993. I'm telling this to you as a negotiator."

Gold also argued that the 2004 exchange of letters between President George W. Bush and Prime Minister Sharon are critical documents in understanding the basis of natural-growth-development issues in international law.[58]

"President Bush's letter dealt with the future territorial contours of an Israeli-Palestinian peace settlement in the West Bank. The letter mentioned two territorial concepts: Under the rubric that Israel will not return to the pre-1967 lines, what are called the 1949 armistice lines, the letter noted there are large Palestinian population centers in the West Bank and that it is unrealistic Israel will pull out of them. That's reference to what is called the 'settlement blocks.'

"The second element is that Israel has a right to what is known as 'defensible borders,' which was a critical term used in Arab-Israeli discussions for many years. The first American to coin the term was President Ronald Reagan in the 1982 Reagan Plan. The original UN Security Council Resolution 242 from 1967 talked about a withdrawal of Israel from territories, but not from all the territories, and acknowledged that Israel had a right to recognized boundaries. Reagan called these boundaries 'defensible borders.' Bush used the term again in the 2004 letter.

"The Bush 2004 letter was essentially a quid pro quo for Israel pulling out of Gaza. Israel got nothing in return from the Palestinians for pulling out, so Israel got its sort of quid pro quo from the United States, which was the Bush letter.

"The Bush 2004 letter was also significant because both houses of the U.S. Congress passed legislation approving the letter. The letter was signed April 14, 2004, and the congressional legislation was taken in June 2004. If you look at the roll call of the vote in the Congress, the vote was overwhelming, by both Republicans and Democrats, including Hillary Clinton, who then was a Democratic senator for New York.[59]

"One of the questions now is whether the Obama administration still sees itself obligated by the 2004 Bush letter," he stressed. "I'm told right now that in Jerusalem there is a growing concern that the Obama administration does not feel bound by the 2004 Bush letter.

"If you have a letter signed by the U.S. president and signed by both houses of Congress, and then the Obama administration says the letter is no longer binding on the United States, what does that mean? We are talking about the fundamental principles upon which international diplomacy is based.

"Richard Holbrooke—the greatest diplomat, in my judgment, of the Clinton years—didn't talk about a peace process, he achieved a peace process—he reached the Dayton Agreement on Bosnia," Gold said with feeling. "Richard Holbrooke would never tear up a previous American understanding with another country.

"Warren Christopher, who worked in both the Carter administration and the Clinton administration, would not do that, either," he continued. "I have a lot of experience with Warren Christopher. He's a lawyer and a very experienced diplomat who also understands these issues.

"So I don't know what is happening under the Obama administration and I don't know who is making these recommendations, but I'm telling you what I believe are the fundamentals of U.S. diplomacy as experienced by Israel for the last fifteen years."

Linkage Between the Israeli-Palestinian Conflict and Iran's Pursuit of Nuclear Weapons

Gold also took issue with any attempt to link the Israeli-Palestinian question to the resolution of Iran's pursuit of nuclear weapons.

"It is broadly asserted by many commentators and some spokespeople for the Obama administration that if Israel would only resolve the Palestinian-Israeli conflict, that would make containment of Iran easier and would help form a coalition of Arab states against Iran," Gold postulated. "This is a baseless argument because countries like the United Arab

Emirates and Saudi Arabia are already threatened by Iran and do not need Palestinian-Israeli diplomacy to get them focused on the issue of Iran developing nuclear weapons.

"Saudi Arabia is not suddenly going to defend its oil-producing regions because Israel pulled up an unapproved outpost on a Sumerian hill," he argued. "Saudi Arabia will defend itself out of Saudi Arabian national security interests. To link the two subjects is simply intellectually groundless."

Gold rejected the validity of any attempt by the Obama administration to delay the settlement of the Iranian nuclear question until a two-state solution has been established with the Palestinians in the Middle East.

"We have gone through six Israeli prime ministers, two American presidents, and two Palestinian leaders in the past few years and no one has solved the Palestinian-Israeli conflict," he pointed out. "Why is it that all of a sudden now we are going to be able to resolve these very difficult issues?

"One of the key questions you have to ask in a conflict before entering diplomacy is 'Do we have here bridgeable differences, or not?'" he pointed out. "With the Palestinian-Israeli conflict, we may right now have unbridgeable differences, such as the division of Jerusalem, or the question of the return of Palestinian refugees. To delay the defense of the oil-producing Arab countries of the Persian Gulf until you solve a problem that may not be soluble in the immediate future is to leave America's Arab allies in the lurch for a very long period of time."

Hamas and Palestinian Authority React to President Obama's Cairo Speech

In the days following President Obama's Cairo speech, the *Jerusalem Post* ran a story titled "Obama-hu akbar!" The story, written by Khaled Abu Toameh, the Palestinian affairs editor for the *Jerusalem Post*, was accompanied by a photograph of two Hamas militants dressed in paramilitary garb, holding automatic weapons and wearing black stocking caps to hide their faces, sitting politely in side-by-side chairs listening attentively to a small color television on which President Obama was seen giving his speech in Cairo. The article ran with a subheadline proclaiming, "The one thing that Fatah and Hamas seem to be able to agree on is their shared sense that U.S. President Barack Obama is good for the Arab and Muslim world in general, and Palestinians in particular." Toameh noted there was "a sigh of relief" among senior Palestinian Authority officials in Ramallah "because, they say, they are no longer facing the same pressure as before."[60]

Toameh quoted one of Abbas's aides after meeting with Mitchell as saying that "the Americans now understand it's Netanyahu who's the obstacle to peace. Netanyahu's refusal to accept the two-state solution and his insistence on building in the settlements are the major threats to peace. We Palestinians, on the other hand, remain committed to the peace process, the two-state solution and to fulfilling all our obligations under the road map." The Abbas spokesman made no reference to the armed Hamas militants pictured by the *Jerusalem Post* listening to President Obama's speech.

What was widely perceived in Israel was that President Obama had reversed U.S. policy to put pressure on Israel. Evidently deciding that Israel was the roadblock to peace in the Middle East, the Obama White House was making clear through the follow-up by Special Envoy Mitchell and Secretary of State Clinton that all settlement developments of any kind would be stopped by Israel immediately, followed by the quick creation of a Palestinian state, whether Israel liked it or not. In Jerusalem, senior Israeli government officials expected pressure to end the blockade and embargo in the Gaza, as a step the United States would require as a precondition for resuming talks with the Palestinian Authority.

In a survey published by the *Jerusalem Post* on June 19, only 6 percent of Jewish Israelis consider the views of American president Barack Obama's administration pro-Israel, a shocking reversal of the trust Jewish Israelis have traditionally put in the commitment of the United States to ensure the survival of the Jewish state.[61]

Hezbollah Fares Poorly in Lebanese Election

In the Lebanese parliamentary election on Sunday, June 7, 2009, just three days after President Obama's speech in Cairo, Hezbollah suffered a major setback in its bid to win enough seats to transform Lebanon into a Hezbollah-controlled state. "If Lebanon becomes a Hezbollah state—that is, a province of Iran controlled by the [Iranian] Revolutionary Guard—then Israel's responses to attacks will no longer distinguish between Hezbollah and Lebanon," an unnamed senior Israeli official told the *Jerusalem Post* only hours before the results of Lebanon's hotly contested parliamentary election were announced. "All Lebanon will be held accountable if Hezbollah takes over."[62]

Surprisingly, the election results showed Hezbollah suffered a setback. The pro-Western March 14 alliance won an unexpected victory over the Hezbollah-led March 8 bloc, with the result that the legislature resulting from the June 7 vote was very similar in representation to the one that preceded it. The election turned on the concerns of Christian Lebanese voters. "Many Lebanese analysts consider that the fears in the [Christian] community over the consequences of a drift further than the Iranian and Syrian regional block played an important part" in Hezbollah's electoral setback, Jonathan Spyer, a senior researcher at the Global Research in International Affairs Center at the Interdisciplinary Center (IDC) in Herzliya, Israel, reported in the *Jerusalem Post*.[63]

The *New York Times* attributed Hezbollah's setback to the impact of President Obama's speech. "President Obama's outreach to the Muslim world seems to have helped undercut the extremists at the polls," a *Times* editorial proclaimed three days after the Lebanese election.[64]

But most Israeli observers discounted the Lebanese

election as having any major impact on Hezbollah. "For Hezbollah and its Iranian patron, the key interest at present is the rebuilding and expansion of its independent military capacity, and the shadow state which has emerged around it," Spyer concluded.

The Visit to Buchenwald

On Friday, June 5, the day after his speech in Cairo, President Obama traveled to Germany to visit the former Buchenwald concentration camp. In doing so, the president bypassed any stopover in Israel. *Haaretz* reported that immediately following the president's Cairo speech, unidentified senior White House officials contacted the newspaper to assert "there is no crisis in our relationship with Israel, and we will succeed in reaching understandings on the matter of settlements."[65] The president toured Buchenwald with Elie Wiesel, who had survived the concentration camp where he had been incarcerated by the Nazis as a teenager. In his remarks, President Obama took exception to Holocaust deniers such as Iranian president Ahmadinejad. "To this day, there are those who insist that the Holocaust never happened—a denial of fact and truth that is baseless and ignorant and hateful," he said. "This is the ultimate rebuke to such thoughts; a reminder of our duty to confront those who would tell lies about our history."[66]

While President Obama's visit to Buchenwald was generally well received in Israel, the visit prompted a closer look at the Cairo speech, in which President Obama had implied that the Holocaust was the reason the State of Israel was created.

In the first days following the Cairo speech and the Buchenwald visit, noted commentators in Israel pointed out that while the Holocaust may have played an important role in President Truman's decision in 1948 to support the creation of the State of Israel, Jewish claims to Israel go back thousands of years.

"By ignoring three thousand years of Jewish history, by neglecting to even mention the unbreakable link, started long before the advent of Islam, between the Jewish people and Eretz Yisrael, Obama totally failed to deliver what should have been one of his most important messages to the Arab world," Dr. Efraim Zuroff, director of the Israel office of the Simon Wiesenthal Center, wrote in the *Jerusalem Post*. "The major problem of the Arab-Israeli conflict and the tensions between Jews and Muslims all over the world is not Holocaust denial. As irritating and disgusting as that phenomenon undoubtedly is, it is merely a symptom of something much deeper, which Obama either failed to understand or refused to understand. And that is the basic refusal of the overwhelming majority of the Muslim world to accept the legitimacy of a Jewish state in the Dar-al-Islam, the Islamic expanse."[67]

The true dilemma President Obama faced was this: How to end the cycle of violence between Israel and its enemies, but also how to create an atmosphere in which forces sworn to destroy Israel will reverse that intention and allow Israel to coexist with them?

FIVE

Prime Minister Netanyahu Responds

In responding to President Obama's Cairo speech, Prime Minister Benjamin Netanyahu faced several hurdles. His administration had been reluctant to embrace a two-state solution largely because Hamas controls the Gaza, effectively negating the ability of the Palestinian Authority to be an effective governmental voice for all Palestinians. Moreover, the increasing pressure of the Obama administration on Israel constituted a threat to the very survival of Netanyahu's government.

Netanyahu's Speech at Bar-Ilan University

On Sunday night, June 14, 2009, two days after the presidential election in Iran, Netanyahu spoke in Hebrew to a national TV audience.

Even the setting of Netanyahu's speech to the nation emphasized the movement of his Likud-led governing coalition to the political right. Bar-Ilan University is Israel's second-largest university. Dedicated to combining Torah studies with general studies, Bar-Ilan was the university attended by Yigal Amir, the extremist Orthodox Jewish student who assassinated Prime Minister Yitzhak Rabin. Yet, at Bar-Ilan University, Netanyahu chose to speak from the Begin-Sadat Center. At the beginning of his speech, Netanyahu commented on this, saying: "We are gathered this evening in an institution named for two pioneers of peace, Menachem Begin and Anwar Sadat, and we share their vision."[68] The comment was designed to call to mind the 1978 Camp David Accords and the 1979 Israel-Egypt Peace Treaty that Prime Minister Begin signed with Egyptian president Anwar Sadat.

In that spirit, Netanyahu said, "I turn to all Arab leaders tonight and I say: Let us meet. Let us speak of peace and let us make peace. I am ready to meet with you at any time. I am willing to meet in Damascus, in Riyadh, in Beirut, anywhere—including Jerusalem." He continued, stressing that he was calling on the Arab countries "to cooperate with the Palestinians and with us to advance an economic peace." Acknowledging that economic peace is not a substitute for political peace, Netanyahu suggested a wide scale of projects for cooperative development, including water desalination, developing solar energy, and laying gas and petroleum lines to link Asia, Africa, and Europe. To the Palestinians, he said, "Let us begin negotiations immediately without preconditions."

Netanyahu strongly disputed the contention that territory was at the heart of the conflict with the Palestinians. "We tried withdrawal with an agreement and withdrawal without an agreement," he said. "We tried a partial withdrawal and a full withdrawal. In 2000 and again last year, Israel proposed an almost total withdrawal in exchange for an end to the conflict, and twice our offers were rejected." Noting that Israel withdrew from the Gaza, uprooted over twenty settlements, and evicted thousands of Israelis from their homes, Netanyahu pointed out that in response Israel "received a hail of missiles on our cities, towns, and children."

"Territorial withdrawals have not lessened the hatred," he concluded. "And to our regret, even Palestinian moderates are not yet ready to say the simple words: Israel is the nation-state of the Jewish people, and it will stay that way." Instead, Netanyahu insisted that "a fundamental prerequisite" for ending the conflict and creating a Palestinian state would be a "binding and unequivocal Palestinian recognition of Israel as the nation-state of the Jewish people." Nor was Netanyahu willing to resolve the Palestinian refugee problem by opening Israel to settlement within its borders by Palestinians claiming a right to return.

While Netanyahu did not reject a two-state solution, he insisted it could be created only on these two key conditions.

He also addressed the issue of the Holocaust, noting that "the right of the Jewish people to a state in the land of Israel does not derive from the cascade of catastrophes that befell our people." Moreover, Netanyahu extended these catastrophes beyond the Holocaust to include a two-thousand-year history in which "the Jewish people suffered expulsions, pogroms, blood libels, and massacres which culminated in the Holocaust, a chain of suffering which has no parallel in history." Then, addressing the Holocaust directly, Netanyahu insisted, "There are those who say that if the Holocaust had not occurred, the state of Israel would never have been established. But I say that if the state of Israel would have been established earlier, it is the Holocaust that would not have occurred." From this, Netanyahu postulated that "the tragic history of powerlessness of our people explains why the Jewish people need a sovereign right of self-defense." That right of self-defense Netanyahu demanded was "*here*, in the land of Israel," the homeland of the Jewish people. "This is where our identity was forged."

With this, Netanyahu left no doubt that resettling Israel in Europe, as Iran's President Ahmadinejad had often suggested, was an unacceptable solution. Without ever mentioning President Obama's comments on the Holocaust in his Cairo speech or the visit to Buchenwald, Netanyahu skillfully repositioned the issue of the Holocaust to leave no doubt that the justification for the Jewish State of Israel did not depend on the atrocities the Nazis committed on European Jews during World War II.

Regarding the creation of a Palestinian state, Netanyahu was specific, presenting his view in terms the White House could not easily dismiss: "In my vision of peace, in this small land of ours, two peoples will live freely, side-by-side, as good neighbors with mutual respect. Each will have its own flag, its own anthem, its own government. Neither will threaten the security or survival of the other."

Still, Netanyahu said he had two conditions: 1) the Palestinians must "clearly and unambiguously recognize Israel as the state of the Jewish people," and 2) the territory under Palestinian control "must be demilitarized with ironclad security provisions for Israel." What Netanyahu said he did not want to see happen was the creation of a Palestinian state "that would become another terrorist base against the Jewish state, such as the one in Gaza."

The following sentence summarized his position: "If we receive this guarantee regarding demilitarization and Israel's security needs, and if the Palestinians recognize Israel as the state of the Jewish people, then we will be ready in a future peace agreement to reach a solution where a demilitarized Palestinian state exists alongside the Jewish state."

Regarding settlements, Netanyahu pledged Israel would not build new settlements or expropriate additional land for existing settlements. Yet Netanyahu would continue natural-growth development in existing settlements, arguing "there is a need to enable the residents to lead normal lives, to allow mothers and fathers to raise their children like families elsewhere."

Reactions to Netanyahu's Bar-Ilan Speech

On behalf of the president, White House Press Secretary Robert Gibbs almost immediately issued a statement saying President Obama "welcomes the important step forward in Prime Minister's Netanyahu's speech."[69] The statement emphasized that President Obama "is committed to two states, a Jewish state of Israel and an independent Palestine, in the historic homeland of both peoples." Read closely, the White House statement appeared to be an implicit acknowledgment of the validity of Netanyahu's argument that the Jewish people had a historic claim on Israel. Moreover, the White House statement implied the Palestinians would have to accept Israel as a Jewish state destined to remain in the Holy Land. The White House showed the first signs of letting Israel up easy, after the hardball negotiations of Special Envoy Mitchell and the uncompromising statements of Secretary of State Clinton.

Palestinian reaction was also immediate: Mustafa Barghouti, a member of the Palestinian Legislative Council, the secretary general of the Palestinian National Initiative, and former candidate for Palestinian president, said the following: "Netanyahu is attempting to mislead the world community by substituting a ghetto for a Palestinian state. He is no partner for peace. His whole speech was nothing but the consolidation of apartheid, not only in the territories but within Israel. Also, he preempted any possibility for negotiations because while he's calling for no preconditions, he is simultaneously saying all of Jerusalem is Israel's capital, there will be no freeze of settlements, and the refugees cannot come home. He's clearly deciding the most important issues while claiming he's open to negotiations."[70]

In Israel, Netanyahu's speech was received favorably, relieving his governing coalition from any immediate internal pressures that might cause the coalition to falter.

Writing in the *Jerusalem Post*, reporter and columnist Caroline Glick called the speech "a positive contribution to the general discourse on the Middle East and Israel's place in it."[71] Glick doubted the speech would have any major impact on the predetermined course the White House had decided to pursue with Israel. Still, she noted that Netanyahu's willingness to accept a two-state solution was designed "to decrease U.S. pressure on his government by conditionally accepting the idea of a Palestinian state." Moreover, Glick felt Netanyahu had demonstrated "that through their consistent rejection of Israel's right to exist as the Jewish state, the Palestinians—not us—are the side responsible for the absence of Middle East peace."

Finally, Glick felt Netanyahu had succeeded in changing Israel's internal dialogue from the tone of the previous Olmert government, which had consistently spoken of the willingness of the Israeli people "to make painful concessions for peace, and treated the establishment of a Jew-free Palestinian state as their primary duty as Zionists." Instead, Glick argued,

"Netanyahu recast the national consensus along patriotic lines."

Regarding natural-growth development in existing settlements, there would still need to be more diplomatic discussion before an effective compromise could be reached. Yet, after Netanyahu's speech at Bar-Ilan University, it was hard to imagine the White House could push unilaterally for the creation of a Palestinian state without taking into consideration more seriously Israel's legitimate national security concerns.

In the final analysis, Netanyahu made it more difficult for the White House to impose on Israel a two-state solution in which Hamas refuses to accept explicitly the existence and survival of Israel as a Jewish state.

How Secure Is Netanyahu's Governing Coalition?

In September 2008, after Kadima's Prime Minister Ehud Olmert was forced to resign in scandal, the number-two Kadima member of the Knesset, Shaul Mofaz, lost by 431 votes a tightly contested Kadima primary in which he challenged then–foreign minister Tzipora "Tzipi" Livni for the leadership of the party.[72]

Mofaz has a thirty-year military history in Israel, including having served as chief of the General Staff of the Israeli Defense Forces. In 2002, under then–Likud prime minister Ariel Sharon, Mofaz served as defense minister. He fought in the 1967 Six-Day War, the 1973 Yom Kippur War, the 1982 Lebanon war, and he was a paratrooper in the Entebbe operation with the elite Special Forces Sayeret Matkal. Sharon had positioned Mofaz as Israel's second most powerful political figure after himself, and he groomed Mofaz to succeed him as the second head of Kadima.

Livni, by comparison, has a reputation for leftist politics and was considered before the February 2009 Israeli parliamentary elections to be a favorite of Israel's print media, much as Democratic Party presidential candidate Barack Obama was the decided favorite of the U.S. mainstream media in the 2008 U.S. presidential election.[73]

Netanyahu became prime minister following the February 2009 Knesset election in which the Kadima party, under Livni's leadership, actually won one more seat than Netanyahu's Likud party. But when Livni was unable to pull together a ruling coalition in the Knesset, President Peres transferred to Netanyahu the opportunity to form a coalition.[74]

By failing to form a government, Livni lost for Kadima the opportunity to continue Olmert's peace process. In retrospect, many of Mofaz's supporters continue to believe he should have demanded a recount of the primary votes after charges arose that voter fraud had been involved in Livni's narrow win. Ironically, whereas the political right wing in the Knesset rejected Livni as future prime minister outright, the same members of the Knesset on the political right would most likely have accepted Mofaz, had he demanded a recount of the primary votes and proven charges that voter fraud was instrumental in Livni's narrow win.

Mofaz, however, had he become the Kadima party prime minister following Olmert, would have deviated most assuredly from Olmert's pursuit of the peace process.[75]

Netanyahu succeeded where Livni had failed, by reaching out to the various parties on the political right, the same strategy Mofaz would have followed.

Critical to forming a governing coalition in the Knesset, Netanyahu forged an alliance with Avigdor Lieberman's Yisrael Beitenu party. Lieberman agreed to become minister of foreign affairs in Netanyahu's government. Lieberman also agreed to serve as one of Israel's four deputy prime ministers.[76]

Netanyahu next managed to convince the Labor party leader and former prime minister, Ehud Barak, to join his government as a deputy prime minister and minister of defense. Netanyahu's governing coalition, however, is considered fragile, especially with Livni waiting in the wings, ready to attempt forming a Kadima government if Netanyahu's coalition begins to falter. Livni refused to join a unity government under Prime Minister Netanyahu, preferring to remain in the opposition.[77]

When the Obama administration pressure on the Netanyahu government built to a high level following the Cairo speech, seasoned observers within Israel speculated that the Obama administration would like to see Netanyahu fail.

A Kadima government headed by Livni was widely

perceived, both in Israel and in the United States, as being more of peace government.[78] Livni was considered ready to pursue Kadima's "convergence plan" in a willingness to disengage unilaterally from parts of the West Bank, following Kadima party prime minister Ariel Sharon's 2005 decision to disengage from Gaza.[79] Conceivably, the West Bank following an Israeli disengagement could have ended up also in the control of Hamas, the same fate that befell Gaza after Israeli disengagement.

The emergence of a political-right coalition in the Knesset following the February 2009 election was considered by many in Israel a major turning point in Israeli politics, signaling a move away from pursuing a peace process in which Israel was required by the United States and the West to cede territory to the Palestinians.

To shore up the Netanyahu coalition, Likud ministers in the Netanyahu government were widely reported in the Israeli press to be courting Mofaz in an effort to persuade him to split away from the opposition faction headed by Livni and join Likud.[80] Mofaz has many friends in Likud and the door appears to remain open to him should he decide to change parties. Whichever way Mofaz plays it, Sharon's desire appears close to being fulfilled, despite the coma that has incapacitated him since 2006. Mofaz is increasingly being seen in the highest circles of Israeli politics as a candidate for Israel's next prime minister to follow Netanyahu. So far, Mofaz has resisted Likud overtures to join the Netanyahu government, not wanting to be opportunistic in his jump back to Likud. In

June 2009, Mofaz preferred to stay put and bide his time as a conservative rival to Livni within Kadima.

Preparing for his June 2009 televised speech to the nation, Netanyahu realized the future of his government depended on his ability to navigate a tight course between the Obama administration pressures and an Israeli electorate moving rapidly to the political right, largely in reaction to the increased threat perceived from Iran and the failure of disengagement from the Gaza to produce peace.[81]

Increasingly, the power broker behind the scenes in Israeli politics is the conservative religious party Shas. Shas won eleven seats in the 2009 elections and decided to join Netanyahu's coalition government after being awarded four cabinet posts. Eliyahu "Eli" Yishai, the spiritual and political leader of Shas, is one of four deputy prime ministers, along with Lieberman and Barak. He is also minister of internal affairs.

Truthfully, given the current composition of the Knesset, it is difficult to imagine Livni ever being able to put together a governing coalition without the approval and involvement of Shas.[82] At present, Shas remains as dedicated an opponent to Livni as is Mofaz behind the scenes. In contrast, Mofaz is well positioned for the future. Mofaz was highly respected by President Bush, Vice President Dick Cheney, and Defense Secretary Donald Rumsfeld, as his policies and actions were closely coordinated with the Bush administration. Any way you look at it, Mofaz is increasingly viewed as Israel's next prime minister after Netanyahu.

SIX

Ahmadinejad Consolidates Power

The inability of the Obama administration or the European Union to intervene in the June 2009 postelection turmoil in Iran provided yet more proof for Ayatollah Khamenei's and President Ahmadinejad's repeated arguments that the United States in particular and the West in general are weak, ready to crumble before the certain triumph of Shiite Islam, just as predicted by Ayatollah Khomeini.

As Khamenei and Ahmadinejad moved to release the Basij and riot police into the streets of Tehran, even the ample citizen-generated news reports circulated on websites such as Twitter, Facebook, and YouTube were not sufficient to mobilize the Obama administration or the EU to intervene. Instead, President Obama and the EU stayed on the sidelines, issuing statements deploring the regime's brutality, statements that the Iranian regime chose to ignore with impunity.

In the final analysis, the street protests offered Khamenei

and Ahmadinejad an opportunity to consolidate their power, a move both eagerly seized.

Iran's Postelection Turmoil Ends Obama Administration Engagement Policy

The postelection turmoil in Iran has clearly derailed any Obama administration plans to engage in direct negotiations with Iran.

The president acknowledged as much when he said at a White House joint press availability with Germany's Chancellor Angela Merkel, "There is no doubt that any direct dialogue or diplomacy with Iran is going to be affected by the events of the last several weeks."[83] Even Iran experts who may have been favorable to the Obama administration have been forced to concur. "The crackdown on protestors has put the possibility of serious negotiations on ice for at least six months, if not for a year," Shaul Bakhash, an Iran expert and history professor at George Mason University, told Gannett News Service.[84]

An article published by the Council on Foreign Relations in the July–August 2009 issue of *Foreign Affairs* may explain why President Obama was reluctant to criticize the Iranian regime for its brutal suppression of the street protests following Iran's June 12 presidential election, as well as why the president's support for the Iranian protestors risking their lives to protest for free elections was so tepid. Writing before the June 12 election in Iran, Mohsen Milani, a politics professor at the University of South Florida, advocated a U.S. strategy of "full engagement" with Iran in an article titled "Tehran's Take: Understanding Iran's U.S. Policy."[85]

A key to the strategy outlined by Milani was that the Obama administration must confer absolute legitimacy on the regime of Ayatollah Khamenei. "As a first step, the United States should allay Iran's fears about regime change," Milani wrote. "It can do this by explicitly recognizing that Khamenei is the center of gravity in Iran's decision-making process and establishing a line of communications with his office."

Milani even suggested a preference that the incumbent president Ahmadinejad should win, despite Ahmadinejad's repeated threats against the survival of Israel. "President Mahmoud Ahmadinejad and his two major reformist rivals, Mir-Hossein Mousavi and Mehdi Karroubi, have all supported engaging in negotiations with Washington—a political taboo just a few years ago," Milani noted. "Ahmadinejad would be less likely to compromise than his more moderate competitors, but, thanks to the support he has among major anti-American constituencies inside and outside the Iranian government, he would be in a better position to institutionalize any shift in policy."

This policy statement almost directly echoes what President Obama said as the postelection street protests in Iran reached their height. "It's important to understand that although there is amazing ferment taking place in Iran, that the difference between Ahmadinejad and Mousavi in terms of their actual policies may not be as great as has been advertised," the president told CNBC, as noted by ABC News senior White House correspondent Jake Tapper.[86] "Either way, we are going to be dealing with an Iranian regime that has historically been hostile to the United States, that has caused some problems in the neighborhood and is pursuing nuclear weapons. And so we've got long-term interests in having them not weaponize nuclear power and stop funding organizations like Hezbollah and Hamas. And that would be true whoever came out on top."

Milani recommended that the Obama administration pursue a strategy of full engagement, "one predicated on gradually increasing economic, educational, and cultural exchanges between the two countries; exploiting the commonalities shared by their governments; and establishing concrete institutional mechanisms to manage their remaining differences."

Curiously, Milani's argument was predicated on perceiving Iran as a typical nation-state that could be understood as motivated by national security interests. Milani decried that little has been written about Iran's policy toward the United States, even though the 2006 National Security Strategy had articulated that the United States faces no greater challenge from a single country than it does from Iran. "What does exist is sensationalistic coverage about Iran's nuclear ambitions and about mad mullahs driven by apocalyptic delusions and a martyr complex," Milani wrote derisively. "In fact, Tehran's foreign policy has its own strategic logic. Formulated not by mad mullahs but by calculating ayatollahs, it is based on Iran's ambitions and Tehran's perception of what threatens them."

Unfortunately for Milani's analysis, what threatened Ayatollah Khamenei was the desire of the Iranian people for free elections. Completely discounted by Milani was the likelihood Iran was developing nuclear weapons not just to gain hegemony in the Middle East, but also to destroy Israel, as Ahmadinejad has so openly proclaimed. Also discounted by Milani and by President Obama was that the Iranian people themselves would perceive an important difference between Mousavi and Ahmadinejad.

What appears naïve after the postelection violence in Iran is any thought that President Obama could now recognize the legitimacy of President Ahmadinejad's reelection in order to enter into direct negotiations with Iran. Should Obama take this route now, he would risk making the issue of Iranian appeasement an issue in the 2010 midterm elections. Like President Carter before him, President Obama risks getting bogged down in pursuing a failed Iran strategy to the detriment of his reelection chances in 2012. Yet, having staked so much on the hope of engagement with Iran, how can President Obama credibly reverse course to embrace the military option?

Meanwhile, Iran continues to make progress on nuclear weapons.

Understanding Ahmadinejad:
A Religious-Radical Traffic Engineer

On January 4, 2006, just six months after taking office, having defeated former president Akbar Hashemi Rafsanjani in a runoff election, President Ahmadinejad held a three-hour closed-door meeting with cabinet members and the Foreign Policy and National Security Committee of the Majlis, Iran's parliament. Here he made a series of statements openly criticizing the foreign policy of his immediate predecessors, presidents Seyed Mohammad Khatami and Rafsanjani. "In the last sixteen years we implemented a policy of détente and tried to get closer to Europe and to trust them," Ahmadinejad noted, "but this policy has achieved nothing." He noted that by the end of Khatami's second term, in 2004, "we were distanced from the goals of the 1979 Islamic revolution and our activity in the Islamic world had been somewhat diminished."[87]

Ahmadinejad was born to a poor family in 1956, in Garmsar, a remote village about fifty-five miles east of Tehran, the fourth of seven children. His family moved to Tehran when he was one year old so his father, a blacksmith who had managed to finish only the sixth grade of elementary education, would have better chances of gainful employment. To help support the family, Ahmadinejad took a job working in a shop that made parts for building cooling systems. "I was a distinguished student," Ahmadinejad writes in the autobiography posted on his website. "The last year of my high school, I prepared myself for the university admission test-conquer [i.e., entrance exam]." In 1976, he entered the Iran University of Science and Technology in Tehran, where he studied civil engineering. In 1997, he got a doctorate from that school in civil engineering and traffic transportation planning.

With the start of the Iran-Iraq War in 1980, Ahmadinejad, then twenty-four years old, rushed to the front. Much remains shrouded in mystery about Ahmadinejad's activities in the 1980s. According to some reports, he joined the Revolutionary Guards Corps (IRGC) in 1986. In the Revolutionary Guards, Ahmadinejad supposedly helped in the kidnapping and assassination of Iranian expatriate dissidents who were considered traitors to the revolution. When the IRGC "al-Quds" (translated, "Jerusalem") Force was founded, Ahmadinejad reputedly became a senior commander, reportedly assigned to direct assassinations in the Middle East and Europe.[88] Other accounts maintain Ahmadinejad was a member only of the Basij, not the more elite Revolutionary Guard.

Before becoming mayor of Tehran in April 2003, Ahmadinejad had served as governor of two small cities in the northwestern province of Kurdistan for two years. In 1993, he was appointed as governor general of the newly established northwestern province of Ardebil, although he was removed by the newly formed "reform" administration of President Khatami. In 1997, he became a member of the scientific board of the Civil Engineering College of the University of Science and Technology. Though he presents himself as a simple man of the people, Ahmadinejad is a highly intelligent individual with extensive practical experience in the daily details of government management.

Many mullahs rode the crest of the revolution to power in Khomeini's theocracy, ending up as millionaires or billionaires, preaching reform and democracy instead of radical revolution. Rafsanjani is the standout case. Rafsanjani began his prerevolutionary career as a peasant pistachio farmer and became an itinerant preacher. The story is widely told of Rafsanjani and his wife hitching rides in the back of trucks traveling from mosque to mosque in the countryside, with his wife hiding the money from the preaching in her garments. Today, billionaire Rafsanjani sports bank accounts around the world and luxury waterfront vacation homes for himself and his family in Dubai. In contrast, Ahmadinejad and his family live in the same small apartment they lived in before he was mayor of Tehran, and Ahmadinejad drives the same auto that was the family car in the years before his rise to power and fame.

The base of Ahmadinejad's political support remains the Basij, the loosely organized and unevenly trained volunteer militia that serves under the direction of the Revolutionary Guards as the street-level morality police throughout Iran, reaching even into small towns and rural communities. The Basij remained loyal to Ahmadinejad during the June 2009 postelection regime violence and they are now recognized worldwide from the citizen-generated video clips showing them riding motorcycles into street protests, beating dissidents at will with their batons.

Ayatollah Yazdi and the Mahdi

Ahmadinejad's chief spiritual adviser is Ayatollah Mohammad Taqi Mesbah Yazdi, known as "the Crocodile" for his rugged facial features and his hard-line orthodox religious views.

Ayatollah Yazdi is the chief living authority on the Mahdi, the "Guided One," better known as the Twelfth Imam or the Hidden Imam. The belief in Shiite Islam is that Muhammad al-Mahdi, the Twelfth Imam in line of succession from the Prophet Muhammad, disappeared down a well in the tenth century A.D., going into "occultation," or hiding, until the appointed time to return. Shiite Muslims believing in the Mahdi maintain that he is a messianic figure who will return after an apocalypse to elevate Shiite Islam to the status of the only true religion, with the consequence that all other false religions, including Sunni Islam, will be vanquished.

A key distinction between Shiite Muslims and Sunni Muslims is that Shiite Muslims believe the legitimate authority over Islam must be established from within Prophet Muhammad's direct family line, whereas Sunni Muslims accept secular leadership, such as the caliphates that ruled Islam during the Ottoman Empire.

Ayatollah Yazdi heads the Imam Khomeini Research and Learning Center in Qom, site of the Jamkaran well, from which Shiite believers expect the Twelfth Imam will reappear. Ayatollah Yazdi has proclaimed that Ahmadinejad is the "chosen" of Imam Mahdi, the person designated to prepare the way for the Mahdi's second coming.[89]

Yazdi is also a member of the Assembly of Experts, the select group of clerics responsible for electing the Supreme Leader from within their ranks. When Ayatollah Khomeini died in 1989, the Assembly of Experts, then chaired by Rafsanjani, elected Ayatollah Khamenei to be the second Supreme Leader.

The informal agreement at the time was that Khamenei would succeed Khomeini, with Rafsanjani becoming president. Key to putting this deal together was Ayatollah Yazdi's support for Khamenei. With his acknowledged years of learning, Ayatollah Yazdi qualifies to be ranked an Imam, a distinction Ayatollah Khamenei does not share. Without Yazdi's support, Khamenei would never have been selected Supreme Leader. Today, Yazdi would have to be considered a possible future Supreme Leader himself, likely to succeed Khamenei.

That Yazdi backed Ahmadinejad was a key factor in determining the latter's electoral victory over Rafsanjani in 2005. In the 2009 presidential election campaign, Rafsanjani was put on notice: during a televised debate with Mousavi, Ahmadinejad directly accused Rafsanjani of corruption, charging that Rafsanjani had enriched himself at the expense of the Iranian people.

When Ayatollah Khamenei declared Ahmadinejad the

winner of the 2009 election, despite protests of voter fraud from Mousavi, the warning was abundantly clear. The first mission would be for the Basij to root out and imprison all known organizers of the street protests. The next mission, once Ahmadinejad was firmly in power and the election protests had been suppressed, would be for Khamenei and Ahmadinejad to turn on Rafsanjani and Mousavi in order to eliminate them as potential rivals in the future.[90]

Earlier in 2009, Ayatollah Yazdi lost a vote to Rafsanjani in a bid to become the head of the Assembly of Experts.[91] Once the postelection protest is completely subdued and Ayatollah Khamenei and President Ahmadinejad have the opportunity to settle all scores against Mousavi and his supporters, another such contest with Rafsanjani may turn out very differently.

Israel Takes Ahmadinejad Seriously

Israeli military intelligence experts are convinced that Ahmadinejad's expressed religious devotion to the Mahdi is genuine.

Equally, Israeli military intelligence takes seriously his repeated threats to destroy Israel. The Jerusalem Center for Public Affairs published in 2008 a detailed examination of Ahmadinejad's menacing public statements. The author, political scientist Joshua Teitelbaum, concluded that the intent of Ahmadinejad's numerous statements calling for the destruction of Israel and the Jewish people was clear. "What emerges from a comprehensive study of what Ahmadinejad actually said—and how it has been interpreted in Iran—is that the Iranian president was not just calling for 'regime change' in Jerusalem, but rather the *actual physical destruction of the State of Israel*," Teitelbaum wrote. "When Ahmadinejad punctuates his speech with 'Death to Israel,' this is no longer open to various interpretations."[92]

As evidence for his conclusions, Teitelbaum published a photograph taken in a military parade in Tehran on September 22, 2003, in which the Iranian regime displayed a Shahab-3 missile inscribed in Farsi with Ahmadinejad's famous statement that "Israel must be uprooted and wiped off [the pages] of history." Evaluating the impact of the image, Teitelbaum wrote, "By juxtaposing its call for Israel's elimination with a Shahab-3 missile during a military parade, the Iranian regime itself has clarified that these expressions about Israel's future do not describe a long-term historical process, in which the Israeli state collapses by itself like the former Soviet Union, but rather the actual physical destruction of Israel as a result of a military strike."[93]

President Ahmadinejad has repeatedly expressed his belief that an imminent apocalypse will be the condition needed to cause the messianic Mahdi to come out of hiding and return to the world.[94] Ahmadinejad has further expressed his belief that the return of the Mahdi will lead to the worldwide triumph of Shiite Islam.[95] Ahmadinejad's beliefs provide a truly frightening threat to the prospect of Israel's survival, especially given the determination with which Iran is pursuing nuclear weapons.

Khamenei Chooses to Go Forward with Ahmadinejad

The idea that Iran has free elections is completely misguided. The Guardian Council in Iran has complete and unquestioned power to decide who may and who may not run for elections for the nation's parliament and presidency.[96] Ahmadinejad won the presidential runoff against Rafsanjani in 2005 because Ayatollah Khamenei wanted Ahmadinejad to win. The same held true for the explanation of why Ahmadinejad beat Mousavi in 2009.

Unlike Ayatollah Khamenei, the Ayatollah Khomeini was revered in Iran and largely throughout the Muslim world because he had accomplished the learning required to be a distinguished Imam. Khomeini was not only a scholar of the Koran, he also was a scholar of ancient Greek philosophy. From Plato, Khomeini took the concept of "Philosopher-King" and elevated it to the key principle of the Iranian theocracy, *Velayet-e Faqih*, which roughly signifies the "Governance of the Jurist."

Put simply, *Velayet-e Faqih* means that the Supreme Leader in the Iranian system is viewed as Allah's divine representative on earth. As such, when the Assembly of Experts selects a Supreme Leader, that body is seen to have discovered and enacted God's judgment, not its own. From this, what follows logically is that the word and decision of the Supreme Leader is by definition the word and decision of Allah on earth. In other words, whatever the Supreme Leader decides is then final, such that anyone who questions the Supreme Leader is not only a traitor but also an apostate.

For this reason, when Mousavi defied the decision of Ayatollah Khamenei that Ahmadinejad won the presidential election, Mousavi was inevitably risking his freedom and possibly even his life in continuing to question Ayatollah Khamenei's authority by insisting that the people of Iran should hold their street protests opposing President Ahmadinejad's victory.

Ayatollah Khamenei was born in 1939 and, like most of the other ayatollahs and mullahs, he is today an old man. However, that some 70 percent of Iranians are under the age of thirty-five and want "hope and change" is irrelevant in the Iranian theocracy.

Truthfully, Ayatollah Khamenei selected Ahmadinejad because Ahmadinejad has the zeal to expand Iran's revolution worldwide. Pragmatically speaking, the only possible conclusion is that the Assembly of Experts, including Ayatollah Yazdi, shares that revolutionary zeal. In other words, Ayatollah Khamenei, the Assembly of Experts, and the Guardian Council have all decided to reelect Ahmadinejad, not *despite* Ahmadinejad's statements that he wants to wipe Israel off the map of the Middle East, but *because* he has said he wants to do so.

That Ayatollah Khamenei brutally suppressed the post-election demonstrations was not only likely, given the Iranian theocracy, it was necessary if the theocracy was to continue to rule.

Now that Ayatollah Khamenei and President Ahmadinejad have consolidated power, they will want to use it—most likely by developing a nuclear weapon to be dropped on Tel Aviv, thereby fulfilling Ahmadinejad's call to destroy Israel.

Why Israel Can't Wait

Ironically, President Obama's weakness in supporting the Iranian postelection street demonstrators makes it more likely Israel will now seriously consider launching a preemptive strike on Iran. U.S. negotiations with Iran could now easily take years; the Iranians could easily take a year simply to talk about talking. With the rapid progress Iran is making on its nuclear program, Israel does not have an indefinite time frame for the United States to resolve the nuclear conflict with Iran.

Israel's Largest Civil Defense Exercise Ever

On Tuesday, June 2, 2009, air raid sirens rang out throughout Israel in Israel's largest-ever civil defense exercise, codenamed "Turning Point 3." On a cloudless day along the Mediterranean beaches in Tel Aviv, a drill was conducted in which schoolchildren were instructed to "duck and cover" under their desks. "Clearly, the drill stimulated the most extreme scenario facing Israel at this point in time—a war on multiple fronts, with Iranian, Syrian, and Hezbollah projectiles, some of them unconventional, raining down on the state," the *Jerusalem Post* wrote.[97] Yet the paper quoted an unnamed "senior defense official" who denied the test had anything to do with a planned Israeli preemptive strike on Iran and the missile retaliation that Iran and her surrogate allies would hurl at Israel in return.

Nevertheless, while defense planners acknowledged that the nationwide drill was the product of the painful learning curve that began with the public unpreparedness for the Hezbollah rocket attacks during the 2006 Second Lebanon War, what was on the mind of millions of Israelis on that Tuesday was that a war with an atomic Iran was suddenly imaginable.

Israel's Nightmare: Atomic Iran

"Since the 1990s, the Iranian leadership decided to acquire military nuclear capability," Vice Prime Minister Yaalon told the author. "The idea was and still is to have a nuclear umbrella under which they will be able to intensify their activities to export the revolution, to undermine moderate regimes in the region, to support and to intensify terror activities, and to gain hegemony. The Iranian leadership is very determined to acquire military nuclear capabilities."

Yaalon pointed out that what the Iranians learned from the decision of President George H. W. Bush to attack Iraq in

1991 was that if Saddam Hussein had gained military nuclear power before the Gulf War, the United States wouldn't have dared to attack it.

Yaalon further argued that Iran's push was to gain hegemony in the Middle East. An atomic Iran would be able to exert considerable muscle over the Middle East, including the ability to impose the will of the Supreme Leader upon the Sunni nations of Egypt, Saudi Arabia, and Jordan.

"So, the whole idea is to challenge not just Israel," Yaalon stressed, "but that Israel should be wiped off the map on the way to defeat the West. It's a misconception to frame the conflict as Iran versus Israel. Israel is only the first step on Iran's way to defeat the United States and the West. Iranian extremists burn the Israeli flag as they burn the American flag. But remember, we are only the Little Satan. The United States is to Iran the Great Satan.

"An atomic Iran will be a nightmare for the international world order, for U.S. and Western interests for the free world, not just for Israel," he asserted. "If Iran gets nuclear weapons, the Egyptians, the Saudi Arabians, the Jordanians, the Turks will follow suit, if only for self-defense.

"The Iranians see in the United States today weakness, a lack of clarity and lack of determination," he continued. "With the United States again talking about talking, the religious clerics ruling Iran see the potential that the Obama administration will pursue appeasement, and concessions are a source of inspiration and encouragement for them.

"The Iranian revolution didn't occur because of Israel," he stressed. "And should Iran manage to wipe Israel off the map, the very next target will be the United States, followed by what the Iranians view as the entire Sunni infidel world. Iranian jihadism is a reality, with or without the State of Israel. Iran, not Israel, is the cause of instability in the Middle East."

At that point, Yaalon made reference to the twelfth-century Torah scholar Moses Maimonides—Rabbi Moshe ben Maimon, known by an acronym in Hebrew, "Rambam."

"We have our Rambam in our Jewish heritage," Yaalon mused. "Rambam said that at the end the truth will show its way. At the end the truth will prevail. If President Obama has a clash with reality in the Middle East, reality will ultimately win out. Unfortunately, somebody is going to pay for it."

Lights Out in the Middle East

Israel is not about to reveal in advance precise military plans for a preemptive attack on Iran. That attack, however, has been thoroughly planned and exercised by Israeli defense intelligence, the Mossad, and the Israeli Defense Forces.

In June 2008, more than one hundred Israeli F-15 and F-16 jet fighters participated in maneuvers over the eastern Mediterranean and Greece that American officials said appeared to be an effort to develop the long-range military capability to strike Iran's nuclear program.[98] In June 2009, Israel sailed a Dolphin-class submarine capable of launching nuclear weapons through the Suez Canal in a move widely seen as a warning to Iran that Israel and Egypt were willing to cooperate against Iran's nuclear threat.[99] On July 5, 2009, the *Sunday Times* in London reported that the head of Mossad has assured Prime Minister Netanyahu that Saudi Arabia would turn "a blind eye" to Israeli jets flying over the kingdom during any future raid on Iran's nuclear sites.[100]

In March 2009, Anthony H. Cordesman, who holds the Arleigh A. Burke Chair in Strategy at the Center for Strategic and International Studies in Washington, D.C., published with CSIS senior associate Abdullah Toukan a 114-page report titled "Study on a Possible Israeli Strike on Iran's Nuclear Development Facilities."[101] Cordesman and Toukan provided a comprehensive analysis of Israel's weapons capabilities and the tactical difficulty of simultaneous military strikes on Iran's multiple nuclear facilities. The authors conclude that an Israeli military strike that would destroy Iran's nuclear facilities or delay the program for some years is possible, though the attack would most likely give rise to regional conflicts and terrorism.

Game planning on a possible Israeli preemptive strike on Iran makes difficult the exact prediction of how the regional conflict would play out. Russia and China are increasingly allied with Iran and neither country would view favorably an Israeli military attack that would further destabilize the Iranian regime. Every day, Iran hardens its nuclear facilities against military attack. In 2008, Russia delivered to Iran twenty-nine Tor-M1 surface-to-air missile systems valued at $700 million; reports continue to circulate that Moscow is contemplating selling Iran its even more sophisticated S300 surface-to-air missile defense system.[102] Ironically, a military attack by Israel might unite the Iranian population to support Ayatollah Khamenei and President Ahmadinejad just when the legitimacy of the regime has faced more popular questioning from within than at any time since the 1979 revolution.

If Israel decides to launch a preemptive strike on Iran's nuclear facilities, it will use the military force judged necessary to accomplish the mission. Israel has the capability, for example, to take out the electricity in wide areas of Iran as preparation for an air and missile attack. With no electricity, Iran would be without cell phones or the Internet, except to the extent military capabilities replaced the deficit. Nor does Israel need to fly over Iraq or Afghanistan, a tactic that would require prior U.S. approval.

While Israel would most likely not use tactical nuclear weapons as a first-strike capability, all of Israel's weapons would be available for use, depending on how the war proceeded.

"Never again!" was the pledge of the European Jews who survived the Holocaust. While Jerusalem's Yad Vashem museum to the Holocaust begins with Hitler's genocidal theories of racial eugenics, the museum ends by chronicling the resistance fighters who took up arms against the Nazis rather than face certain death passively. The 1943 Warsaw Ghetto uprising marked a turning point in Jewish history, when Jews realized defense rested in their own hands and fighting back was eminently doable.

"Never again!" remains the motto of the Jewish government leaders whom I met with in Israel in May and June 2009. The Jews today governing Israel will not stand by helplessly while the world frets over what to do about yet another rogue regime that threatens to annihilate Jews.

None of this is to say that Israel is enthusiastic about launching a preemptive strike against Iran. To the contrary, Israel's attacking Iran would be a version of what has been called the "Samson Option," a reference to Samson bringing down the temple to kill the enemy Philistines even though the action caused his own death. If Israel's government approves the attack, Israel will have reached the conclusion that even a war with uncertain chances of success, certain chances of retaliation, and unknown risks of escalation will be better than doing nothing.

While Israel's top leaders are frank in acknowledging that a preemptive attack on Iran may be unavoidable if the United States is unable to stop Iran's progress with nuclear weapons, this does not mean that Israel's leaders believe a war with Iran will be easy or certain of success. Israel is well aware that a war with Iran would involve retaliation not only from Iran, but also from Iran's terrorist surrogates, Hezbollah and Hamas. Civilian casualties in Israel are certain to be high from the missile and rocket attacks that Iran, Hezbollah, and Hamas could send upon Israel. In a war with Iran, no one in Israel will be safe, not even in Jerusalem. Conceivably, one-third of the Israeli population could be killed or wounded in an all-out war with Iran. Civilian losses of this magnitude are horrifying to conceptualize, especially for military planners and government leaders charged with the responsibility for preserving, protecting, and defending the State of Israel.

Still, in the final analysis, Israel is a "one bomb" state such that one atomic bomb, even of a relatively low yield, detonated successfully over Tel Aviv, Israel's business, banking, and telecommunications center, would destroy the modern Jewish state as the world knows it. If Israel decides that an atomic Iran makes the annihilation of Israel certain, even the horror of taking massive civilian casualties makes self-defense necessary. Even if self-defense necessitates that Israel must launch a preemptive attack on Iran, using the military option will be Israel's last resort.

Why Can't Israel Wait?

Unfortunately, the time is growing short. Iran will soon be able to develop its first deliverable nuclear weapon.

Terrorists typically do not stockpile weapons—they use them. With Iran's stated intention to wipe Israel off the map, Israel cannot afford to take the risk.

Notes

Preface: Israel's Right of Self-Defense

1. Moshe Yaalon, interview with author, Jerusalem, June 14, 2009.

2. Jerome R. Corsi, *Atomic Iran: How the Terrorist Regime Bought the Bomb and American Politics* (Nashville, Tenn.: WND Books, 2005).

3. Michael D. Evans with Jerome R. Corsi, *Showdown with Nuclear Iran: Radical Islam's Messianic Mission to Destroy Israel and Cripple the United States* (Nashville, Tenn.: Nelson Current, 2006).

Chapter 1: Postelection Turmoil in Iran

4. Ali Akbar Dareini and Brian Murphy, "Iran's leader: End protests or risk 'bloodshed,'" Associated Press, June 19, 2009, at http://www.breitbart.com/article.php?id=D98U0H8O1&show_article=1.

5. Damien McElroy, "Profile: Mir-Hossein Mousavi, Iran's presidential challenger," *Telegraph*, June 18, 2009, at http://www.telegraph.co.uk/news/worldnews/middleeast/iran/5566463/Profile-Mir-Hossein-Mousavi-Irans-presidential-challenger.html.

6. Jeff Stein, "Mousavi, Celebrated in Iranian Protests, Was the Butcher of Beirut," CQ Politics, June 22, 2009, at http://

blogs.cqpolitics.com/spytalk/2009/06/mousavi-celebrated-in-iranian.html?referrer=js.

7. President Ronald Reagan, press conference, December 17, 1981, at http://www.reagan.utexas.edu/archives/speeches/1981/121781c .htm.

8. President Barack Obama, "Remarks by the President on a New Beginning: Cairo University, Cairo, Egypt," White House, June 4, 2009, at http://www.whitehouse.gov/the_press_office/ Remarks-by-the-President-at-Cairo-University-6-04-09/.

9. "Sen. McCain Takes Administration to Task on Iran," *Your World with Neil Cavuto*, Fox News, June 22, 2009, at http:// www.foxnews.com/story/0,2933,528127,00.html.

10. Michael Weissenstein and Anna Johnson, "Amateur video turns woman into icon of Iran unrest," Associated Press, June 22, 2009, at http://news.yahoo.com/s/ap/20090622/ap_on_re_ mi_ea/ml_iran_election_icon.

11. Lara Setrakian, ABC News, on Twitter.com, June 22, 2009, at http://twitter.com/LaraABCNews/statuses/2279312682.

12. Martin Fletcher, "Iran admits 50 cities had more votes than voters," TimesOnLine, June 22, 2009, at http:// www.timesonline.co.uk/tol/news/world/middle_east/ article6553843.ece.

13. Images were posted by Bultan News at BultanNews.com.

14. CNN/YouTube Democratic Presidential Debate Transcript, CNN, posted July 24, 2007, at http://www.cnn.com/2007/ POLITICS/07/23/debate.transcript/index.html.

15. Barbara Slavin, "Exclusive: U.S. contacted Iran's ayatollah before election," *Washington Times*, June 24, 2009, at http:// www.washingtontimes.com/news/2009/jun/24/us-contacted- irans-ayatollah-before-election/?feat=home_cube_position1.

16. Exclusive Interview with Harry Smith, "Obama: Can't Let U.S. Be 'Foil' for Tehran," CBS News, June 22, 2009, at http://www. cbsnews.com/stories/2009/06/22/earlyshow/main5102053 .shtml.

17. Scott Peterson, "Iran blames U.S. for 'intolerable' meddling," *Christian Science Monitor*, June 17, 2009, at http://www.csmonitor.com/2009/0618/p06s04-wome.html.

18. Jay Solomon, Jonathan Weisman, and Yochi J. Dreazen, "Obama Rips Iran in Tactical Shift," *Wall Street Journal*, June 24, 2009, at http://online.wsj.com/article/SB124575867345041295.html.

Chapter 2: Iran's Nuclear Weapons Program

19. "Iran 'would like nuclear option,'" BBC News, June 17, 2009, at http://news.bbc.co.uk/2/hi/middle_east/8104388.stm.

20. National Intelligence Estimate, "Iran: Nuclear Intentions and Capabilities," November 2007, at http://www.dni.gov/press_releases/20071203_release.pdf.

21. Statements of the Director, "Intervention on Non-Proliferation Issues at the IAEA Board of Governors by IAEA Director General Dr. Mohamed ElBaradei," IAEA Board of Governors, Vienna, Austria, June 17, 2009, at http://www.iaea.org/NewsCenter/Statements/2009/ebsp2009n007.html#iran.

22. Danny Yaton, interview with the author, Tel Aviv, June 11, 2009.

23. Shabtai Shavit, interview with the author, Tel Aviv, May 28, 2009.

24. William J. Broad and David E. Sanger, "Iran Has More Enriched Uranium Than Thought," *New York Times*, February 19, 2009, at http://www.nytimes.com/2009/02/20/world/middleeast/20nuke.html.

25. William J. Broad and David E. Sanger, "Iran Has Centrifuge Capacity for Nuclear Arms, Report Says," *New York Times*, June 5, 2009, at http://www.nytimes.com/2009/06/06/world/middleeast/06nuke.html.

26. Ali Akbar Dareini, "Iran tests missile with range that can hit Israel," Associated Press, May 20, 2009, at http://www.breitbart.com/article.php?id=D98A4CQG2&show_article=1.

27. Alon Ben-David, "Iran unveils redesigned Shahab missile," *Jane's Defense Business News*, September 27, 2004, at http://www .janes.com/aerospace/military/news/jdw/jdw040927_1_n.shtml.

28. "Q&A: Iran and the nuclear issue," BBC News, May 22, 2009, at http://news.bbc.co.uk/2/hi/middle_east/4031603.stm.

29. Committee on Foreign Relations, U.S. Senate, "Iran: Where We Are Today," Letter of Transmittal signed by Committee Chairman Sen. John F. Kerry, May 4, 2009 (Washington, D.C.: U.S. Government Printing Office, 2009), p. 5, at http://74.125.47.132/search?q=cache:qYhXNwjCffQJ:foreign .senate.gov/Iran.pdf+senate+report+%2B+%22Iran:+Where+ Are+We+Today%3F%22&cd=1&hl=en&ct=clnk&gl=us.

30. Ibid., p. 1.

31. Tribune Staff Report, "Media questions, Obama answers," *Chicago Tribune* Transcript, November 8, 2008, at http://www .chicagotribune.com/chi-obama-transcript-1107,0,939229 .story.

32. The White House, Office of the Press Secretary, "Remarks by President Obama and Prime Minister Netanyahu of Israel in Press Availability," May 18, 2009, at http://www.whitehouse .gov/the_press_office/Remarks-by-President-Obama-and- Israeli-Prime-Minister-Netanyahu-in-press-availability/.

Chapter 3: Hezbollah, Hamas, and Syria

33. Dr. Reuven Erlich, biographical note, International Institute for Counter-Terrorism, at http://www.ict.org.il/Biographies/ DrReuvenErlich/tabid/190/Default.aspx.

34. Dr. Reuven Erlich, interview with author, Tel Aviv, June 4, 2009.

35. "Exporting the Iranian Revolution to Lebanon," Intelligence and Terrorism Information Center, Tel Aviv, Israel, December 8, 2008, at http://www.terrorism-info.org.il/malam_multimedia/ English/eng_n/html/iran_e003.htm.

36. "Hamas sweeps to election victory," BBC News, January 26, 2006, at http://news.bbc.co.uk/2/hi/middle_east/4650788 .stm.

37. "Remarks by President Obama and President Abbas of the Palestinian Authority in Press Availability," White House, May 28, 2009, at http://www.whitehouse.gov/the_press_office/ Remarks-by-President-Obama-and-President-Abbas-of-the-Palestinian-Authority-in-press-availability/.

38. Lieutenant General (ret.) Moshe Yaalon, "Foreword: Iran's Race for Regional Supremacy," in *Iran's Race for Regional Supremacy: Strategic Implications for the Middle East* (Jerusalem: Jerusalem Center for Public Affairs, 2008), at http://www.jcpa .org/JCPA/Templates/showpage.asp?DBID=1&LNGID=1& TMID=84&FID=452&PID=2280, pp. 6–13, at p. 8.

39. Ibid.

40. Ibid., p. 11.

41. Ibid., p. 6.

42. For a technical description of the Iranian-made Zelzal rocket, see "Zelzal-2/Mushak-200," GlobalSecurity.org, at http:// www.globalsecurity.org/wmd/world/iran/zelzal-2.htm.

43. Alistair Lyon, "ANALYSIS—Hezbollah chief stirs Arabs to turn on rulers," Reuters, December 30, 2008, at http:// uk.reuters.com/article/idUKLU87392.

44. Howard Schneider, "Gazans Hope U.S. Leader Pushes Israel to Relax Grip," *Washington Post*, May 16, 2009, at http://www .washingtonpost.com/wp-dyn/content/article/2009/05/15/ AR2009051503606.html.

45. Anna Fifield, "Hezbollah confirms broad aid for Hamas," *Financial Times*, May 12, 2009, at http://www.ft.com/cms/ s/0/1ee8637e-3eee-11de-ae4f-00144feabdco.html.

46. Haaretz Service, "Syria threatens to take back Golan by force," Haaretz.com, June 28, 2009, at http://www.haaretz.com/ hasen/spages/1095962.html.

47. James Rosen, "Obama to Return U.S. Ambassadors to Syria, Venezuela," Fox News, June 24, 2009, at http://www.foxnews .com/politics/2009/06/24/obama-return-ambassador-syria/.

48. "Assad and Ahmadinejad discuss joint U.S. strategy," *Syria Today*, no. 50, June 2009, at http://www.syria-today.com/ index.php?option=com_content&view=article&id=1692: assad-and-ahmadinejad-discuss-joint-us-strategy&catid=29: news&Itemid=28. See also Agence France Presse, "Ahmadinejad, Assad vow support for resistance," May 6, 2009, at http:// www.dailystar.com.lb/article.asp?edition_id=10&categ_ id=2&article_id=101696.

49. Associated Press, "Assad: Syria-Iran ties serve stability and strength of Mideast," May 6, 2009, at http://www.haaretz.com/ hasen/spages/1083216.html.

Chapter 4: President Obama in Cairo

50. Herb Keinon, "Jerusalem warily applauds Obama's speech," *Jerusalem Post*, June 4, 2009, at http://www.jpost.com/servlet/ Satellite?cid=1244034998681&pagename=JPost%2FJPArticle %2FShowFull.

51. All references in this section to President Obama's speech in Cairo are drawn from the following source: President Barack Obama, "Remarks by the President on a New Beginning: Cairo University, Cairo, Egypt," White House, June 4, 2009, at http://www.whitehouse.gov/the_press_office/Remarks-by- the-President-at-Cairo-University-6-04-09/.

52. See, for instance, "Clinton urges Israel settlement halt, no exception," Reuters, May 27, 2009, at http://www.reuters.com/ article/vcCandidateFeed1/idUSTRE54Q5DG20090527.

53. White House, Office of the Press Secretary, "Remarks by President Obama and Prime Minister Netanyahu of Israel in Press Availability," May 18, 2009, at http://www.whitehouse .gov/the_press_office/Remarks-by-President-Obama-and- Israeli-Prime-Minister-Netanyahu-in-press-availability/.

54. U.S. Department of State, "Secretary of State Hillary Clinton: Press Availability with Egyptian Foreign Minister Ahmed Ali Aboul Gheit," May 27, 2009, at http://www.state.gov/secretary/rm/2009a/05/124009.htm.

55. Herb Keinon, "Mitchell: US and Israel 'remain close allies and friends,'" *Jerusalem Post*, June 9, 2009, at http://www.jpost.com/servlet/Satellite?cid=1244371046239&pagename=JPost%2FJPArticle%2FShowFull.

56. Jonathan Tobin, "Which side are they on?" *Jerusalem Post*, June 6, 2009, at http://www.jpost.com/servlet/Satellite?cid=1244035011468&pagename=JPost%2FJPArticle%2FShowFull.

57. Ambassador Dore Gold, interview with the author, Jerusalem, June 1, 2009.

58. "Exchange of letters between PM Sharon and President Bush," Israel Ministry of Foreign Affairs, April 14, 2004, at http://www.mfa.gov.il/MFA/Peace+Process/Reference+Documents/Exchange+of+letters+Sharon-Bush+14-Apr-2004.htm.

59. See "House, Senate Back Sharon Disengagement (June 23–24, 2004)," Jewish Virtual Library, at http://www.jewishvirtuallibrary.org/jsource/US-Israel/hconres460.html.

60. For the Internet version of the story, with a different headline than the version of the story published in the newspaper, see Khaled Abu Toameh, "Palestinian Affairs: Our man in Washington?" *Jerusalem Post*, June 11, 2009, at http://www.jpost.com/servlet/Satellite?cid=1244371076584&pagename=JPost%2FJPArticle%2FShowFull.

61. Gil Hoffman, "'Jerusalem Post'/Smith Poll: Only 6% of Israelis see US government as pro-Israel," *Jerusalem Post*, June 19, 2009, at http://www.jpost.com/servlet/Satellite?pagename=JPost%2FJPArticle%2FShowFull&cid=1245184872947.

62. Haviv Rettig Gur and Associated Press, "All Lebanon will be held accountable if Hezbollah takes over," *Jerusalem Post*, June 8, 2009.

63. Jonathan Spyer, "Analysis: Lebanon election results offer some relief, but no major changes," *Jerusalem Post*, June 8, 2009, at

http://www.jpost.com/servlet/Satellite?cid=1244371045793&
pagename=JPost/JPArticle/ShowFull.

64. "Editorial: Lebanon's Election," *New York Times*, June 10, 2009,
at http://www.nytimes.com/2009/06/11/opinion/11thu2.html.

65. Barak Ravid, "Post-Obama speech, U.S. seeks to reduce Israel
tensions," Haaretz.com, June 5, 2009, at http://www.haaretz
.com/hasen/spages/1090537.html.

66. Posted by Kevin Hechtkopf, "Transcript: Obama, Merkel and
Wiesel at Buchenwald," CBS News, June 5, 2009, at http://www
.cbsnews.com/blogs/2009/06/05/politics/politicalhotsheet/
entry5066311.shtml.

67. Efraim Zuroff, "Analysis: What Obama failed to understand,
or refused to publicly identify," June 4, 2009, *Jerusalem Post*, at
http://www.jpost.com/servlet/Satellite?pagename=JPost%2FJ
PArticle%2FShowFull&cid=1244035002248.

Chapter 5: Prime Minister Netanyahu Responds

68. Prime Minister Benjamin Netanyahu, Prime Minister's Office,
"Speech at the Begin-Sadat Center at Bar-Ilan University," June
14, 2009, at http://www.pmo.gov.il/PMOEng/Communication/
PMSpeaks/speechbarilan140609.htm.

69. "White House reacts to Netanyahu's speech," CNN Political
Ticker at CNNPolitics.com, June 14, 2009, at http://
politicalticker.blogs.cnn.com/2009/06/14/white-house-
reacts-to-netanyahus-speech/.

70. "Netanyahu Speech: Palestinian Reaction," Sabbah Blog,
June 15, 2009, at http://sabbah.biz/mt/archives/2009/06/15/
netanyahu-speech-palestinian-reaction/.

71. Caroline Glick, "Our World: Obama's losing streak and us,"
Jerusalem Post, June 15, 2009, at http://www.jpost.com/servlet/
Satellite?pagename=JPost%2FJPArticle%2FShowFull&
cid=1244371106195.

72. "Livni wins Israel primary," BBC News, September 18, 2008, at http://news.bbc.co.uk/2/hi/middle_east/7620215.stm.

73. "Study Shows Printed Media Bias Favors Livni," Arutz Sheva, Israel National News, August 28, 2008, at http://www .israelnationalnews.com/News/Flash.aspx/152085.

74. Linda Gradstein, "Netanyahu to Form Israeli Government," *Washington Post*, February 21, 2009, at http://www .washingtonpost.com/wp-dyn/content/article/2009/02/20/ AR2009022000219.html.

75. Author's interviews with member of the Knesset Shaul Mofaz in Israel, June 2009.

76. Rory McCarthy, "Hardliner Avigdor Lieberman set to become Israel's foreign minister," *Guardian*, March 16, 2009, at http:// www.guardian.co.uk/world/2009/mar/16/avigdor-lieberman-israel.

77. *Jerusalem Post* Staff and Gil Hoffman, "Netanyahu-Livni meeting unfruitful," *Jerusalem Post*, February 27, 2009, at http://www.jpost.com/servlet/Satellite?cid=1235410730954& pagename=JPost%2FJPArticle%2FShowFull.

78. Attila Somfalvi, "Livni: No unity government under current terms," YNetNews.com, March 16, 2009, at http://www .ynetnews.com/articles/0,7340,L-3687302,00.html.

79. Pierre Atlas, "Israel's New Government: What a Difference Three Years Makes," Real Clear Politics, March 27, 2009, at http://www.realclearpolitics.com/articles/2009/03/israels_ new_government_what_a.html.

80. Mazal Mualem, "Likud courting Kadima's Mofaz," *Haaretz*, May 28, 2009, at http://www.haaretz.com/hasen/spages/1088473 .html.

81. Gil Hoffman, "Politics: Between Barack and a hard place," *Jerusalem Post*, June 11, 2009, at http://www.jpost.com/servlet/ Satellite?pagename=JPost%2FJPArticle%2FShowFull& cid=1244371077184.

82. See, for instance, Gwen Ackerman and Alisa Odenheimer, "Lieberman, Shas Back Netanyahu as New Israeli Premier," Bloomberg.com, February 19, 2009, at http://www.bloomberg.com/apps/news?pid=20601087&sid=aSipp.L5iDOo&refer=home.

Chapter 6: Ahmadinejad Consolidates Power

83. "Obama: violence harms dialogue with Iran," UPI.com, June 26, 2009, at http://www.upi.com/Top_News/2009/06/26/Obama-violence-harms-dialogue-with-Iran/UPI-59701246047884/.

84. "Turmoil in Iran Undercuts Obama Outreach," Gannett News Service, July 1, 2009, at http://www.jaxobserver.com/2009/07/01/turmoil-in-iran-undercuts-obama-outreach/.

85. Mohsen M. Milani, "Tehran's Take: Understanding Iran's U.S. Policy," *Foreign Affairs*, July/August 2009, pp. 46–62, at http://www.foreignaffairs.com/articles/65123/mohsen-m-milani/tehrans-take.

86. Jake Tapper, "President Obama: On Key Policies, Not Much Difference Between Ahmadinejad and Mousavi," ABC News, June 17, 2009, at http://blogs.abcnews.com/politicalpunch/2009/06/president-obama-not-much-difference-between-ahmadinejad-and-mousavi.html.

87. Iran Focus, "Iran's president criticizes détente foreign policy," IranFocus.com, Jan. 3, 2006, at http://www.iranfocus.com/modules/news/article.php?storyid=5117.

88. Information on the background of Mahmoud Ahmadinejad in this and the following paragraph is drawn from "Mahmoud Ahmadinejad: Biography," at http://www.globalsecurity.org/military/world/iran/ahmadinejad-bio.htm.

89. Iran Press Service, "Iran Government Urging the Hidden Imam to Help," Iran-Press-Service.com, October 21, 2005, at http://www.iran-press-service.com/ips/articles-2005/october-2005/jamkaran_211005.shtml. See also Amir Taheri, *The Persian*

Night: Iran under the Khomeinist Revolution (New York and London: Encounter, 2009), pp. 80–82.

90. For an excellent analysis of how Ayatollah Yazdi plays into 2009 postelection Iranian politics, see Muhammad Sahimi, "The Leaders of Iran's 'Election Coup,'" Tehran Bureau, June 16, 2009, at http://tehranbureau.com/the-leaders-of-iran%E2%80%99s-election-coup/.

91. Mazyar Mokti and Charles Recknagel, "How Could Iran's Hard-Liners Choose the Next Supreme Leader?" Radio Free Europe/Radio Liberty, July 5, 2009, at http://www.rferl .org/content/How_Could_HardLiners_Choose_The_Next_ Supreme_Leader/1769299.html.

92. Joshua Teitelbaum, *What Iranian Leaders Really Say About Doing Away with Israel: A Refutation of the Campaign to Excuse Ahmadinejad's Incitement to Genocide* (Jerusalem: Jerusalem Center for Public Affairs, 2008), at http://www.jcpa.org/text/ ahmadinejad2-words.pdf, p. 5.

93. Ibid., p. 13.

94. See, for instance, James Zumwalt, "For Iran, It's Apocalypse Now," *Human Events*, May 27, 2009, at http://www .humanevents.com/article.php?id=32009.

95. For a discussion of the return of the Mahdi and the triumph of Shiite Islam, see Vali Nasr, *The Shia Revival: How Conflicts Within Islam Will Shape the Future* (New York: Norton, 2006), p. 67.

96. See, for instance, "Guardian Council," in the BBC News, "Iran: Who holds the power?," at http://news.bbc.co.uk/2/shared/spl/ hi/middle_east/03/iran_power/html/guardian_council.stm.

Conclusion: Why Israel Can't Wait

97. Yaakov Lappin, "Security and Defense: Cause for Alarm?" *Jerusalem Post*, June 6, 2009, at http://www.jpost.com/servlet/ Satellite?cid=1244035011450&pagename=JPost%2FJPArticle %2FShowFull.

98. Michael R. Gordon and Eric Schmitt, "U.S. Says Israeli Exercise Seemed Directed at Iran," *New York Times*, June 20, 2008, at http://www.nytimes.com/2008/06/20/washington/20iran .html.

99. Yehudah Lev Kay, "Israeli Sub Sails Through Suez Canal, Sending Warning to Iran," *Arutz Sheva*, Israel National News, July 5, 2009, at http://www.israelnationalnews.com/News/ News.aspx/132206.

100. Uzi Mahnaimi and Sarah Baxter, "Saudis give nod to Israeli raid on Iran," *Sunday Times*, July 5, 2009, at http://www.timesonline .co.uk/tol/news/world/middle_east/article6638568.ece.

101. Anthony H. Cordesman and Abdullah Toukan, "Study on a Possible Israeli Strike on Iran's Nuclear Development Facilities," March 14, 2009, at www.csis.org/files/media/csis/ pubs/090316_israelistrikeiran.pdf.

102. Tony Halpin and Alexi Mostrous, "Russia ratchets up US tensions with arms sales to Iran and Venezuela," *London Times*, September 19, 2008, at http://www.timesonline.co.uk/tol/ news/world/europe/article4781027.ece.